Sacrifice

SACRIFICE

THE LEGACY OF OUR BELOVED PROPHET ﷺ

A Compilation of Ḥadīth About the Struggles and Hardships of Our Beloved Prophet ﷺ

By Tameem Ahmadi

NUR PUBLICATIONS

ISBN: 978-1-7338110-0-2 (paperback)
ISBN: 978-1-7338110-1-9 (hardback)

Library of Congress Control Number: 2019903152

Nur Publications
P.O. Box 97
Union City, CA
United States of America

www.nurpublications.org

First edition: November 2016
Second edition: April 2019

Design, Editing & Cover by: Nur Publications

Front Calligraphy by Adil Mohamady
*"And those who struggle in Our cause,
surely We shall guide them in Our ways."* (Qur'ān 29:69)

Questions

If you have any questions regarding the subject matter contained in any of our books, please email us at *questions@nurpublications.org* and *inshā-Allah* a member of our staff will reach out to you.

Corrections

No one is perfect, but Allah. If you find any mistakes in our books please email us at *corrections@nurpublications.org*.

Printed by Mega Printing in Turkey

Dedication

I dedicate this book

To my Master, my Teacher & my Mentor...

To the coolness of my eyes & the contentment of my heart...

To the one whose intercession I yearn for...

To the Paragon of all virtue...

To the Leader of all mankind...

To the Imam of all the Prophets & Messengers...

To the Beloved of Allah...

MUḤAMMAD, THE SON OF ʿABDULLAH

صلى الله عليه وآله وسلم

Transliteration and Honorific Guide

The transliteration used in our books is to facilitate the pronunciation of Arabic words using Roman script for the ease and convenience of our readers. However, this is not meant to be a substitute for learning to properly read and pronounce Arabic script. Every Muslim should take it upon themselves to learn the rules of *tajwīd* (proper Qurʾānic recitation) from a qualified teacher.

أ,ء	a, ʾ	ط	ṭ	ُ	u
ب	b	ظ	ẓ	آ,ـَا	ā
ت	t	ع	ʿ	ـِي	ī
ث	th	غ	gh	ـُو	ū
ج	j	ف	f	ﷻ	"Glorified and Exalted"
ح	ḥ	ق	q		
خ	kh	ك	k	ﷺ	"Peace and blessing of Allah be upon him"
د	d	ل	l		
ذ	dh	م	m		"Peace be upon him/them"
ر	r	ن	n		
ز	z	و	w		"Allah be pleased with him/her"
س	s	ه	h		
ش	sh	ي	y		"Allah be pleased with them"
ص	ṣ	َ	a		"Allah have mercy upon him"
ض	ḍ	ِ	i		

According to the convention used in our books:

-The Majestic Name, "Allah," does not take a diacritic.

-The *tā marbūtah* (ة) that occurs at the end of some Arabic words is generally transliterated into English with an "h" at the end of the word, except when it comes in the names of people in which case it is dropped off.

-Arabic words transliterated into English are italicized except words that have been adopted into the English dictionary, commonly used words, and proper nouns.

Contents

کلمات بابرکات

از سیّدي و سندي حضرت مولانا شاہ محمد قمر الزمان صاحب دامت برکاتھم

بسمہ تعالی

ما شاء اللہ اس کو پڑھا، بہت مفید و مبارک مجموعہ ہے جو عموماً عوام تو عوام، خواص کو بھی پیش نظر نہیں ہے، جبکہ ایسی احادیثِ رقاق کی طرف دعوت اور انکی تعلیم و تبلیغ کا سلسلہ عام ہونا چاہیے. اللہ تعالی مزید اصلاحی مضامین و مقالات کے پیش کرنے کی توفیق نصیب فرمائے۔ آمین۔ و باللہ التوفیق .

و السلام

محمد قمر الزمان الہ آبادي

(دامت برکاتھم)

A Word of Blessing and Encouragement

In the Name of Allah

I have read (the Arabic text of) this book and found it to be a very beneficial and blessed compilation of ḥadīth. Notwithstanding the average Muslim, even some of those with proficiency in Islamic knowledge often forget these ḥadīths. These heart-softening ḥādīths should be propagated and taught more frequently. May Allah bless you with the ability to produce more works related to the reformation of the self. Amīn and with Allah is our tawfīq.

Was Salām,

(Haḍrat Mawlānā Shāh)

Muḥammad Qamaruz-Zamān Ilāhabādī

30th of Muḥarram, 1427 — 1st of November, 2016
Bayt al-Adhkār, Wasiyabād,
Ilāhabād, UP India

بسم الله الرحمن الرحيم

Introduction

THE GREATEST OF ALL JOURNEYS IS THAT WHICH leads to our Beloved Allah. It is the very purpose of our existence. And yet, as in all journeys, there will definitely be hardship. In the face of these difficulties, the *nafs* at times becomes weak and courage starts to wane. However, in every journey there are guides who have knowledge of the way. They lead the wayfarer to salvation through their guidance and experience. Their courage inspires us, and through this inspiration, we can find our way through the wilderness of this world and reach our destination: total submission and devotion to the Beloved, Allah Most High.

Our guides in this world are the prophets, martyrs, and saints. Their lives enlighten us. Their words inspire us. Their examples and stories uplift our spirits.

Allah ﷻ mentions in the Qur'ān:

﴿وَكُلًّا نَّقُصُّ عَلَيْكَ مِنْ أَنۢبَآءِ ٱلرُّسُلِ مَا نُثَبِّتُ بِهِۦ فُؤَادَكَ ۚ وَجَآءَكَ فِى هَٰذِهِ ٱلْحَقُّ وَمَوْعِظَةٌ وَذِكْرَىٰ لِلْمُؤْمِنِينَ﴾

"And all that We relate to you of the stories of the Messengers is that by which We strengthen your heart. In these [verses] there has come to you truth and an admonition, and a reminder for the believers."

(Qur'ān 11:120)

Imām Abū Ḥanīfa said, "Relating stories and anecdotes of the saintly scholars regarding their excellent character and conduct is more beloved to me than most discussions of *fiqh*,[1] because in these stories lie the very principles of the *qawm*.[2]

1 This refers to the Islamic laws of jurisprudence, or the technical laws and tenets of Islam that pertain to external matters.

2 "Principles of the *qawm*" refers to the etiquettes and manners of the pious predecessors.

Imām Abū 'l-Qāsim Junayd ﷺ said, "Stories (of the pious) are the armies of Allah ﷻ by which He strengthens the hearts of the believers." He then recited:

﴿وَكُلًّا نَّقُصُّ عَلَيْكَ مِنْ أَنۢبَآءِ ٱلرُّسُلِ مَا نُثَبِّتُ بِهِۦ فُؤَادَكَ﴾

"And all that We relate to you of the stories of the Messengers is that by which We strengthen your heart..."

(Qur'ān 11:120)

If the stories of the Messengers strengthen the hearts of the believers, then the story of the Master and Leader of all Messengers is the greatest of stories.

The Messenger of Allah ﷺ himself advises his Ummah[3] with these profound words, spoken during his final illness:

يَا أَيُّهَا النَّاسُ، مَنْ أُصِيبَ مِنْكُمْ بِمُصِيبَةٍ مِنْ بَعْدِي فَلْيَتَعَزَّ بِمُصِيبَتِهِ بِي عَنْ مُصِيبَتِهِ الَّتِي تُصِيبُهُ فَإِنَّهُ لَنْ يُصَابَ أَحَدٌ مِنْ أُمَّتِي مِنْ بَعْدِي بِمِثْلِ مُصِيبَتِهِ بِي

3 His community, those that believe in him and follow in his footsteps until the Last Day.

> "O People! Any of you who is afflicted by a calamity after my demise, then let him seek patience [by reminding himself] of the calamity of my passing, for verily no one from my Ummah will ever be afflicted by a calamity greater than the calamity of my demise."[4]

Even though this ḥadīth is referring specifically to comparing one's own calamity to the calamity of the Messenger's *demise*, we can also take solace from *all* his sacrifices and hardships. For indeed, his hardships were like mountains compared to ours.

Ultimately, whatever suffering or difficulty we experience in this life utterly dissolves in the face of the difficulty of losing the Messenger of Allah ﷺ. The Messenger's presence in this world was a "mercy for all the worlds"; his heart was the place upon which revelation descended; and through his presence, humanity was blessed with such guidance and faith that allowed them to endure *all* calamities and finally find complete rest in the eternal company of their Lord. Even if the Prophet ﷺ is no longer with us physically, his teachings remain with us, and we are being taught that in difficult times, we should bring to mind his passing, and this will immediately place our current difficulty into perspective.

---

[4] Ibn Mājah and Ṭabarānī

The poet, Abū 'l-'Atāhiya said so beautifully:

لَنَا فِكْرَةٌ فِي أَوَّلِينَا وَعِبْرَةٌ   بِهَا يَقْتَدِي ذُوالْعَقْلِ مِنَّا وَيَهْتَدِي

لِكُلِّ أَخِي ثُكْلٍ عَزَاءٌ وَأُسْوَةٌ   إِذَا كَانَ مِنْ أَهْلِ التُّقَى فِي مُحَمَّدِ

There is a reminder and lesson for us
in our predecessors to take heed of,

Which the intelligent among us follow
and are guided by;

For every grieving person there is
solace and example...

If he is from the people of piety
in the example of Muḥammad!

In this compilation, I present some of the struggles that our Beloved Messenger ﷺ endured in the various aspects of his life: spiritual, physical, mental, and emotional.

As we are reading these incidents from the life of our Beloved Messenger ﷺ, we should reflect upon them and compare our difficulties to his difficulties, our pain to his pain. We should ponder over how he struggled for the sake of his Lord to fulfill His commandments, convey the message revealed to him, and please his Lord. Through these reflections, we will inevitably arrive at the conclusion that our hardships are nothing compared to his; that our pain is insignificant when measured against what he experienced. Nevertheless, we can learn how to navigate through our own difficulties by following his ﷺ beautiful example. If we want to learn about how to handle life's challenges in a way that is pleasing to Allah ﷻ and draws us closer to Him, what better example than that of His Beloved Messenger?

May Allah ﷻ shower His eternal blessings and mercies upon him perpetually, for eternity, according to His glory and honor. May Allah make this book a source of guidance and inspiration for all those who read it and may He accept it out of His sheer Mercy. *Āmīn*.

Tameem Ahmadi
Fremont, California
14th of Safar, 1437
14th of November, 2016

SACRIFICES IN THE PERSONAL LIFE OF THE BELOVED PROPHET

صلى الله عليه وآله وسلم

مجاهدته ﷺ في الزهد عن لذّات الدنيا

His ﷺ Struggles in Abstaining From Worldly Pleasures

Ḥadīth 1

[عَنْ أَبِي أُمَامَةَ الْبَاهِلِيّ رضي الله عنه] عَنِ النَّبِيّ ﷺ قَالَ: عَرَضَ عليَّ رَبِّي لِيَجْعَلَ لِي بَطْحَاءَ مَكَّةَ ذَهبًا، فَقُلْتُ: لَا يا ربِّ ولَكِنْ أَشْبَعُ يومًا وَأَجُوعُ يَوْمًا - أَوْ قَالَ ثَلَاثًا أَوْ نَحْوَ هذا - فَإِذَا جُعْتُ تَضَرَّعْتُ إِلَيْكَ وَذَكَرْتُكَ، وَإِذَا شبِعْتُ شَكَرْتُكَ وَحَمِدْتُكَ.

(رواه أحمد والترمذي وقال الترمذي: هذا حديث حسن)

Abū Umāma al-Bāhilī رضي الله عنه narrates:

The Messenger of Allah ﷺ said, "My Lord offered to turn the valley of Makkah into gold for me, to which I replied, 'No, my Lord. Rather, I wish to eat to my fill one day and stay hungry one day; so that when I am hungry, I will implore You and remember You, and when I am full, I will praise You and be grateful to You.'"

(Tirmidhī and Aḥmad)

COMMENTARY

The great Master of Ḥadīth, Mullā ʿAlī Qārī ؒ, writes, "Know that the abstinence and poverty of the Prophet ﷺ was voluntary; it was not brought upon him through compulsion and it continued till the day of his demise."[5] In other words, the Prophet ﷺ did not abstain from worldly pleasures simply because of his circumstances, rather he chose a life of simplicity and austerity for specific reasons.

Some of the reasons mentioned by commentators are:

• Out of mercy for the weak and poor of his Ummah.

• To be an example and role model for them in how to exercise patience in difficulties.

• To prove the superiority of the spiritual state of the poor patient man over the rich grateful man.

Allah ﷻ states:

﴿وَلَا تَمُدَّنَّ عَيْنَيْكَ إِلَىٰ مَا مَتَّعْنَا بِهِۦٓ أَزْوَٰجًا مِّنْهُمْ زَهْرَةَ ٱلْحَيَوٰةِ ٱلدُّنْيَا لِنَفْتِنَهُمْ فِيهِ ۚ وَرِزْقُ رَبِّكَ خَيْرٌ وَأَبْقَىٰ﴾

---

[5] *Jamʿ al-Wasāʾil*

And do not extend your glance toward what We have given to some of them to enjoy, from the splendor of the life of this world through which We test them: but the provision of Your Lord is better and more enduring.

(Qurʾān 20:131)

It is from the perfection of a leader and a testament to his acumen that he takes into consideration the weakest of his people. This is one of the reasons why the life of the Prophet ﷺ is, in and of itself, one of the proofs of his prophethood.

Another reason for the Prophet's ﷺ choice of poverty is, as he himself proclaims, "I wish to eat to my fill one day and stay hungry one day, so that I may be patient and grateful." In this way, he was able to join between the two states of *shukr* and *ṣabr*,[6] which are the two primary avenues of drawing close to Allah. Through his voluntary hunger and destitution, he manifested the perfection of his relationship with Allah Most High. Ultimately, this ḥadīth captures the intimate conversation between the lover and the Beloved. In essence, Allah ﷻ is asking the Messenger of Allah ﷺ, "What do you want, the life of this world or Me?" And the Messenger ﷺ is

---

6 *Shukr* (gratitude) and *ṣabr* (patience) are the two essential pathways to The Beloved, great and glorious is He. In times of ease, one shows gratitude to Allah, and in times of difficulty one is patient with His decree, staying steadfast on what He has commanded. The Messenger of Allah ﷺ encompassed both these ranks simultaneously.

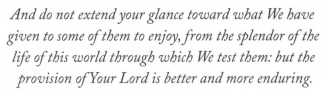

responding with humility that he desires nothing but the pleasure of his Beloved Allah.

HADĪTH 2

عَنْ عَائِشَةَ ﵂ قَالَتْ: قَالَ رَسُولُ اللهِ ﷺ: يَا عَائِشَةُ لَوْ شِئْتُ
لَسَارَتْ مَعِي جِبَالُ الذَّهَبِ، جَاءَنِي مَلَكٌ إِنَّ حُجْزَتَهُ لَتُسَاوِي
الْكَعْبَةَ، فَقَالَ: إِنَّ رَبَّكَ يَقْرَأُ عَلَيْكَ السَّلَامَ، وَيَقُولُ لَكَ: إِنْ شِئْتَ
نَبِيًّا عَبْدًا، وَإِنْ شِئْتَ نَبِيًّا مَلِكًا. قَالَ: فَنَظَرْتُ إِلَى جِبْرِيلَ قَالَ:
فَأَشَارَ إِلَيَّ أَنْ ضَعْ نَفْسَكَ. قَالَ: فَقُلْتُ: نَبِيًّا عَبْدًا. قَالَ: فَكَانَ
رَسُولُ اللهِ ﷺ بَعْدَ ذَلِكَ لَا يَأْكُلُ مُتَّكِئًا يَقُولُ: آكُلُ كَمَا يَأْكُلُ
الْعَبْدُ، وَأَجْلِسُ كَمَا يَجْلِسُ الْعَبْدُ.

(رواه أبو يعلى وحسّنه الهيثمي)

ʿĀʾISHA ﵂ NARRATES THAT THE MESSENGER OF ALLAH ﷺ SAID:

O ʿĀʾisha! If I had wished, mountains of gold would have followed me. Such an angel came to me that the height of his mere waistband matched the size of the Kaʿbah. This angel said, "Your Lord conveys His *salām* to you and asks, 'Do you wish to be a slave-prophet or a king-prophet?'" I looked towards Jibrīl and he made a gesture to me to be humble. I then responded, "I wish to be a slave-prophet."

ʿĀʾisha ◈ states that after this incident, the Messenger of Allah ﷺ would not eat reclining. Instead, he would say, "I eat just as a slave eats and I sit just as a slave sits."

(Abū Yaʿlā)

COMMENTARY

Throughout history there were either prophets who were kings, like the Prophets Dāwūd and Sulaymān ◈, or prophets who were slaves who lived in austerity, like the Prophets ʿĪsa and Yaḥya ◈. None of the other Prophets were bestowed both bounties and given a choice other than our Master Muḥammad ﷺ.[7]

We see in the above-mentioned ḥadīth that after the Prophet ﷺ chose the path of slavehood and austerity, he immediately adjusted certain aspects of his life—he would not sit reclining

---

[7] Imām al-Suyūṭī indicates to this in his *Khaṣāʾiṣ al-Kubrā*, wherein he relates six ḥadīths in this regard. See *Khaṣāʾiṣ*.

during meals and adopted utter humility in all his actions. This indicates that the path we choose in life comes with practical implications. In other words, when we say we are Muslims, it means we must also live as practicing Muslims.

Likewise, if Allah ﷻ has blessed us with knowledge, we should adopt the demeanor and noble habits of the scholars and the righteous. If Allah blesses us with children, we must choose the path of being positive role models for them. If we are running institutes or organizations, we must be responsible leaders and deal with fairness, equity, and trustworthiness.

We can learn many lessons from these ḥadīths wherein Allah is giving the Prophet ﷺ an option of how to live. Everything he did and all the choices he made were reflective of his rank of utmost servitude, slavehood, and humility before Allah. Whether it was his eating, sitting, sleeping, bedding, or overall lifestyle—all of it reflected slavehood and humility.

As a leader and role model for all of humanity, had he chosen the lifestyle of a king and adopted the path of affluence, his example would not have been universal. It would have served as an example for the wealthy alone, excluding the weak and the poor. By choosing a life of austerity, his lifestyle earned the admiration of the rich and exemplified solidarity with the poor.

صفة خُشُونة حصيره وَوِسادته ﷺ

The Description of the Roughness of the Prophet's ﷺ Spread and Pillow

Ḥadīth 3

قَالَ عُمَرُ بْنُ الْخَطَّابِ رضي الله عنه: جِئْتُ فَإِذَا رَسُولُ اللهِ ﷺ فِي مَشْرُبَةٍ
له (أَيْ غُرْفَةٍ) ... وَإِنَّهُ لَعَلَى حَصِيرٍ مَا بَيْنَهُ وَبَيْنَهُ شَيْءٌ، وَتَحْتَ
رَأْسِهِ وِسَادَةٌ مِنْ أَدَمٍ حَشْوُهَا لِيفٌ، وَإِنَّ عِنْدَ رِجلَيْهِ قَرَظًا
مَصْبُورا، وَعِنْدَ رَأْسِهِ أَهَبٌ مُعَلَّقَةٌ، فَرَأَيْتُ أَثَرَ الْحَصِيرِ فِي جَنْبِهِ
فَبَكَيْتُ فَقَالَ: مَا يُبْكِيكَ؟ فَقُلْتُ: يَا رَسُولَ اللهِ! إِنَّ كِسْرَى
وَقَيْصَرَ فِيمَا هُمَا فِيهِ، وَأَنْتَ رَسُولُ اللهِ. فَقَالَ رَسُولُ اللهِ ﷺ:
أَمَا تَرْضَى أَنْ تَكُونَ لَهُمُ الدُّنْيَا وَلَنَا الْآخِرَةُ؟

(رواه البخاري ومسلم واللفظ للبخاري)

ʿUmar ibn al-Khaṭṭāb رضي الله عنه narrates:

I came to the Messenger of Allah ﷺ and found him in his room... lying down on a straw mat with nothing between him and the mat. He had a pillow under his head that was made of leather and stuffed with palm fibers. Gathered by his feet was some bark for tanning. Hanging by his head were some leather water bags. I saw marks on his side from the straw mat, and I began to weep. He asked, "Why are you crying?" I replied, "O Messenger of Allah, the emperors of Persia and Rome both enjoy luxurious living while you, being the Messenger of Allah, are in this condition!" He ﷺ then replied, "Are you not pleased [knowing] that the life of this world is for them, while for us is the everlasting hereafter?"

(Bukhārī and Muslim)

Commentary

ʿUmar ؓ is describing the scene in detail so that the humble state in which he saw the Messenger of Allah ﷺ can be fully conveyed to us.

From this incident, we can learn what the proper perspective of a believer should be. We are grateful for whatever worldy luxuries Allah grants us, while remaining mindful that the pleasures and luxuries of this life are only temporary. The real life and pleasure we seek are in the hereafter.

Allah ﷻ says:

﴿وَمَا هَٰذِهِ ٱلۡحَيَوٰةُ ٱلدُّنۡيَآ إِلَّا لَهۡوٞ وَلَعِبٞۚ
وَإِنَّ ٱلدَّارَ ٱلۡأٓخِرَةَ لَهِيَ ٱلۡحَيَوَانُۚ لَوۡ كَانُواْ يَعۡلَمُونَ﴾

What is the life of this world but amusement and play?
Surely the next life is indeed the true life;
if only they knew.

(Qurʾān 29:64)

ḤADĪTH 4

عَنْ عَبْدِ اللهِ بن مسعود رضي الله عنه قَالَ: نَامَ رَسُولُ اللهِ ﷺ عَلَى حَصِيرٍ، فَقَامَ وَقَدْ أَثَّرَ فِي جَنْبِهِ، فَقُلْنَا: يَا رَسُولَ اللهِ لَوِ اتَّخَذْنَا لَكَ وِطَاءً، فَقَالَ: مَا لِي وَمَا لِلدُّنْيَا، مَا أَنَا فِي الدُّنْيَا إِلَّا كَرَاكِبٍ اسْتَظَلَّ تَحْتَ شَجَرَةٍ ثُمَّ رَاحَ وَتَرَكَهَا.

(رواه الترمذي وقال: وفي الباب عن ابْنِ عُمَرَ، وَابْنِ عَبَّاسٍ، هَذَا حَدِيثٌ حسن صَحِيحٌ.)

ʿAbdullah ibn Masʿūd ؓ narrates:

> The Messenger of Allah ﷺ was sleeping on a straw mat. As he arose, the imprint of the mat was visible on his side. We said, "O Messenger of Allah! May we get proper bedding for you?" He replied, "What do I have to do with this world? I am but like a traveler in this world who seeks shade under a tree, and then departs and leaves it behind."
>
> (Tirmidhī)

Commentary

The key point to take into consideration here is the example the Messenger of Allah ﷺ left for his Companions and his Ummah—the example of *zuhd* (abstinence from the world). The life of this world is even more temporary than a brief stop that a traveler takes under a tree to rest. If we ponder over this reality, all the difficulties of life and the stressful situations we experience will begin to seem insignificant.

With that being said, there is a very important point for us to understand. After reading these ḥadīths, the thought may come to one's mind that perhaps it is sinful to live in comfort, to have soft bedding, to eat delicious food, or to enjoy the luxuries of life. This is an incorrect notion. These ḥadīths are not asking us to abandon the lawful pleasures of life.

Allah ﷻ says:

﴿يَٰبَنِيٓ ءَادَمَ خُذُواْ زِينَتَكُمۡ عِندَ كُلِّ مَسۡجِدٖ وَكُلُواْ وَٱشۡرَبُواْ وَلَا تُسۡرِفُوٓاْۚ
إِنَّهُۥ لَا يُحِبُّ ٱلۡمُسۡرِفِينَ ۝ قُلۡ مَنۡ حَرَّمَ زِينَةَ ٱللَّهِ ٱلَّتِيٓ أَخۡرَجَ لِعِبَادِهِۦ
وَٱلطَّيِّبَٰتِ مِنَ ٱلرِّزۡقِۚ قُلۡ هِيَ لِلَّذِينَ ءَامَنُواْ فِي ٱلۡحَيَوٰةِ ٱلدُّنۡيَا خَالِصَةٗ يَوۡمَ
ٱلۡقِيَٰمَةِۗ كَذَٰلِكَ نُفَصِّلُ ٱلۡأٓيَٰتِ لِقَوۡمٖ يَعۡلَمُونَ﴾

O Children of Ādam! Put on your beautiful clothing at every time and place of prayer: Eat and drink, but waste not by excess: For Allah does not like the wasters. Say: "Who has forbidden the beautiful (gifts) of Allah, which He has made for His slaves, and (those) clean and pure things He provided, for living?" Say: "In the life of this world, they are for those who believe, (and only) purely for them on the Day of Judgment: Thus We explain the Signs in detail for those who understand."

(Qur'ān 7:31–32)

The purpose of these ḥadīths is essentially to demonstrate the status of the Messenger's slavehood and humility. He ﷺ deliberately preferred such a lifestyle for the reasons we have already mentioned. If living an austere life of complete abstinence was demanded from us, then why is it that

Companions such as Abū Bakr al-Ṣiddīq, ʿUthmān ibn ʿAffān, ʿAbd al-Raḥmān ibn ʿAwf, Saʿd ibn Abī Waqqāṣ, Ṣakhr ibn Widāʿa al-Ghāmidī along with many of the Anṣār of Madīnah ﷺ, were known to possess tremendous wealth, date gardens, and livestock?

In fact, if it weren't for the financial assistance of the affluent Companions, the great military expeditions would not have been funded. Furthermore, their charitable contributions made it possible for the poor and needy to be supported, and for many slaves to be emancipated. On many occasions, the Messenger of Allah ﷺ prayed for them and even gave them glad tidings of Paradise due to their selfless generosity. How could this have ever been achieved if they had abandoned all worldly occupations?

Hence, we realize that lawful worldly pleasures are not evil in and of themselves, but are only evil if they are acquired through forbidden means, spent on unlawful things, or squandered in vanity. Understand this well.

صفة أكله وطعامه ﷺ

Description of His ﷺ Eating and Meals

Ḥadīth 5

عَنِ النُّعْمَانِ بْنِ بَشِيرٍ رضي الله عنه قَالَ: أَلَسْتُمْ فِي طَعَامٍ وَشَرَابٍ مَا شِئْتُمْ؟ لَقَدْ رَأَيْتُ نَبِيَّكُمْ ﷺ وَمَا يَجِدُ مِنَ الدَّقَلِ مَا يَمْلَأُ بِهِ بَطْنَهُ. وَقُتَيْبَةُ لَمْ يَذْكُرْ: بِهِ، وَفِي رِوَايَةٍ: وَمَا تَرْضَوْنَ دون ألوانِ التَّمرِ والزُّبدِ.

(رواه مسلم)

Nuʿmān ibn Bashīr رضي الله عنه said [to some of the people of his time]:

Do you not have all that you desire of food and drink? Indeed, I have seen your Prophet ﷺ [in a state where] he did not even have the lowest quality of dates by which he could fill his stomach.

In another narration, it is mentioned, "You people, on the other hand, are not satisfied unless you have a variety of dates and butter."

(Muslim)

Commentary

These days we become agitated and bitter when things don't go our way (for instance, when we don't get the exact type of food we like). If we are invited to a place as a guest and only one type of food is prepared, or there is only one dish, we consider it to be dishonorable and complain that it was a lousy invitation.

Living pampered lives, we have become intolerant of even the slightest inconveniences. This attitude has ruined our character as Muslims. It has turned us into eating machines whose greatest concern in life is tantalizing our senses.

The purpose of reading such ḥadīths is to overcome these negative characteristics, to develop qualities that are beloved to Allah, to increase in gratitude and contentment for whatever Allah has blessed us with, and, finally, to remain pleased with Allah's decree in all circumstances.

The point here is not to say that enjoying a variety food is *ḥarām*. Rather, Nuʿmān ibn Bashīr ﵁ is encouraging those around him who had not witnessed the life of the Prophet ﷺ to be grateful and content with what Allah has given them. If we are not satisfied with whatever Allah has given us, we should remember the Messenger's life.

In a narration of *Ṣaḥīḥ Muslim*, the Messenger of Allah ﷺ advised us, "Look to those who are lesser than you [in their worldly means], and do not look to those who are higher than you [in their worldly means]. That is more appropriate, so that you do not consider Allah's bounties upon you as insignificant."

HADĪTH 6

عَنْ عُرْوَةَ عَنْ عَائِشَةَ ﵂ أَنَّهَا قَالَتْ لِعُرْوَةَ: إِبْنَ أُخْتِيْ، إِنْ كُنَّا لَنَنْظُرُ إِلَى الْهِلَالِ، ثُمَّ الْهِلَالِ، ثَلَاثَةَ أَهِلَّةٍ فِيْ شَهْرَيْنِ، وَمَا أُوْقِدَتْ فِيْ أَبْيَاتِ رَسُوْلِ اللّٰهِ ﷺ نَارٌ. فَقُلْتُ: يَا خَالَةُ، مَا كَانَ يُعِيْشُكُمْ؟ قَالَتْ: اَلْأَسْوَدَانِ التَّمْرُ وَالْمَاءُ، إِلَّا أَنَّهُ قَدْ كَانَ لِرَسُوْلِ اللّٰهِ ﷺ جِيْرَانٌ مِنَ الْأَنْصَارِ، كَانَتْ لَهُمْ مَنَائِحُ، وَكَانُوْا يَمْنَحُوْنَ رَسُوْلَ اللّٰهِ ﷺ مِنْ أَلْبَانِهِمْ فَيَسْقِيْنَا.

(رواه البخاري ومسلم واللفظ للبخاري)

ʿURWA IBN AL-ZUBAYR NARRATES:

ʿĀʾisha ﵂ said to [me], "O my nephew! We used to see the new moon, then another new moon—three moons in two months, and not a single fire was lit in the houses of the Messenger of Allah ﷺ." I asked, "O my aunt! Then what were your means of sustenance?" She replied, "Dates and water. However, the Messenger of Allah ﷺ had neighbors from the Anṣār who owned milk-giving goats or camels and they would send some of the milk from their animals to the Messenger of Allah ﷺ, which he would serve to us."

(Bukhārī and Muslim)

Commentary

The ḥadīth indicates that the stove would not be lit for two months in a row. In other words, they would not have any cooked food to eat for that length of time.

The Messenger of Allah's ﷺ life is an example even for those who are suffering through the severest difficulties. Be it our brothers and sisters in refugee camps, or others in extreme need—everyone can look at the life of the Prophet ﷺ and witness a beautiful example of patience and contentment in Allah's decree. Truly the Prophet of Allah ﷺ was a role model for people from every spectrum of life.

دعاؤه ﷺ لأهله ليجعل الله رزقهم كفافاً

His ﷺ Prayer for His Household That Allah Make Their Sustenance the Bare Minimum

HADĪTH 7

عَنْ أَبِي هُرَيْرَةَ قَالَ، قَالَ رَسُوْلُ اللهِ ﷺ: اللّٰهُمَّ اجْعَلْ رِزْقَ آلِ محمدٍ قُوتًا.

(رواه مسلم)

Abū Hurayra ؓ narrates:

> The Messenger of Allah ﷺ said, "O Allah! Make the provisions of the family of Muḥammad just enough to suffice them."

(Muslim)

Commentary

The meaning of *"qūt"* in this duʿāʾ is: that level of sustenance whereby one has just enough to survive. What boggles the mind is that this is a duʿāʾ that a father is making for his family!

This ḥadīth demonstrates the deep recognition that the Messenger of Allah ﷺ had of the reality of this world. He was fully aware that anything more than what fulfills one's needs can easily throw a person headlong into heedlessness and vanity. For this reason, his duʿāʾ is ultimately a duʿāʾ of mercy.

In a narration found in Bukhārī and Muslim, he ﷺ said, "[O my Ummah], it is not poverty that I fear for you, rather I fear that the [temptation of the] life of this world opens itself up to you like it did for the people before you. I am afraid that you will compete in its acquisition just like they did; and it will destroy you as it destroyed them."

We learn from these words of wisdom that whatever suffices us for our needs is better than that abundance which makes us heedless of Allah.

Allah ﷻ says:

﴿ أَلْهَىٰكُمُ ٱلتَّكَاثُرُ ۝ حَتَّىٰ زُرْتُمُ ٱلْمَقَابِرَ ﴾

"Competing in amassing (worldly means) has distracted you, until you reach the graves..."

(Qurʾān 102:1–2)

The Messenger of Allah ﷺ mentioned in a ḥadīth narrated in Tirmidhī, "Hasten to do good deeds before seven things come upon you…" One of the things he then listed was, "… wealth that makes you rebellious [against Allah]…"

We should observe how our hearts react to the above ḥadīths. If our hearts and minds are imbued with materialism and obsession for amassing wealth, we will be blind to the benefit in these narrations; the very idea of living with "just enough" will make us cringe out of nervousness.

Fear of poverty—considering poverty to be a curse from God—is a sickness of the heart. Likewise, being obsessed with amassing wealth, competing with others in this regard, or thinking that this is what brings about status and virtue is also a grave deception. On the other hand, working for the necessities of life and fulfilling one's family responsibilities is an honorable matter and an act of devotion to Allah. The lesson we learn from this prayer of the Messenger of Allah ﷺ for his family is that wealth is a virtue as long as it fulfills one's needs and necessities; however, anything beyond that can become a slippery slope.

Commentators say that the word *"āl"* in this ḥadīth—normally translated as "family"—can have an array of meanings and interpretations. According to some scholars, *"āl"* may also refer to those who are his lovers and followers.

One poet says:

آلُ النَّبِيِّ هُمْ أَتْبَاعُ مِلَّتِهِ   عَلَى الشَّرِيْعَةِ مِنْ عُجْمٍ وَمِنْ عَرَبِ

لَوْ لَمْ يَكُنْ آلُهُ إِلَّا قَرَابَتُهُ   صَلَّى الْمُصَلِّي عَلَى الطَّاغِي أَبِيْ لَهَبِ

The Āl of the Prophet ﷺ *are the adherents*
and followers of his nation,

Who adhere to the Sharīʿah
whether they be ʿArab or ʿAjam;[8]

If his Āl were only those of his family,

Then we would also be reciting salutations
upon the tyrant—Abū Lahab!

So even though the Prophet ﷺ made this supplication specifically for his immediate family, if you find yourself having "just enough" to get by in life, then consider it not a sign of misfortune; rather hope for it to be a sign of your spiritual proximity to the Noble Messenger ﷺ and his honorable family.

---

8 Meaning non-Arab.

شدّ الأحجار على بطنه الشريف من شدّة ألم الجوع

The Tying of Stones to His ﷺ Blessed Stomach Due to Severe Pangs of Hunger

Ḥadīth 8

عَنْ أَنَسِ بْنِ مَالِكٍ رضي الله عنه، عَنْ أَبِي طَلْحَةَ، قَالَ: شَكَوْنَا إِلَى رَسُولِ اللهِ ﷺ الْجُوعَ وَرَفَعْنَا عَنْ بُطُونِنَا عَنْ حَجَرٍ حَجَرٍ، فَرَفَعَ رَسُولُ اللهِ ﷺ عَنْ حَجَرَيْنِ.

(رواه الترمذيّ)

Anas ibn Mālik narrates from Abū Ṭalḥa رضي الله عنه:

We complained to the Messenger of Allah ﷺ of hunger and raised [our garments] from our stomachs, exposing the stones that were tied to them. The Messenger of Allah ﷺ then raised [his garment], revealing *two* stones.

(Tirmidhī)

Commentary

The background of this ḥadīth is that it took place during the Battle of Khandaq.[9] It was very cold, the Ṣaḥābah were ill-equipped, and they were all very hungry. Their hunger had reached such an extent that they had to tie something to press against their stomachs from the outside to alleviate the pangs of hunger. Mullā ʿAlī Qārī writes in his *Mirqāt* that it was a known practice among the people of Madinah to fasten stones to one's stomach when experiencing severe pangs of hunger.

Tying stones around the belly placed pressure on the stomach, and this would reduce the sensation of emptiness that resulted in severe hunger pangs.

This ḥadīth shows again how our Beloved Prophet ﷺ was a step ahead in everything—even in his enduring hardship in the path of Allah. This also shows the quality of a true leader:

---

9. The Battle of Khandaq (the Trench), also known as the Battle of Aḥzāb (the Joint-Armies), occurred in the fifth year after Hijra. The Quraysh joined forces with the tribe of Ghaṭfān and with financial support from the Jewish tribes of Khaybar formed an army of 10,000 men and marched upon Madīnah. Having only 3,000 able-bodied men to defend the city, the Messenger of Allah ﷺ ordered the Muslim army to dig a large trench as a defensive ploy to keep the larger army at bay. It was hard, painstaking work at a time when food was scarce and the weather was frigid. However, with the help of Allah the strategy proved successful; after laying siege to the city for nearly a month, the army of the disbelievers retreated.

he suffers twice the amount of his followers. He ﷺ was the first and foremost in doing what needed to be done, thereby setting an example for all of his followers. Contrast his example to that of the so-called leaders of today, who sit in comfort and send the common man off to die for their greedy, materialistic motives.

Shaykh al-Ḥadīth Mawlānā Muḥammad Zakariyya Kāndhlawī writes in his commentary on the *Shamāʾil*:

> ...The fastening of stones was out of sympathy; to join the poor and needy by becoming a part of them. As a general rule, when the seniors [of a group] experience some hardship, their juniors do not feel so affected in their own difficulties. In this case, what could be said of the Companions of the Prophet ﷺ, whose love for the Messenger of Allah ﷺ knew no bounds? When they saw his pain and the stones tied to his noble stomach, they completely forgot their own plight.
>
> When the Ṣaḥābah would experience great poverty and hunger—even reaching a stage where stones had to be fastened to their stomachs—the Messenger of Allah ﷺ did not take the benefit of special favors, like asking Allah to nourish him, while his Companions suffered; whereas we know that Allah would provide nourishment to the Prophet ﷺ while he fasted continuously. [It would not have been difficult for Allah

to provide for the Messenger ﷺ in the same way during this battle.] However, just as a mother would find it difficult to eat her food knowing that her child suffers from hunger, what could be said about the Messenger of Allah ﷺ, when his love for the Ummah exceeded the love of a thousand mothers?

الخروج من البيت من شدة الجوع

Leaving the House Due to Excessive Hunger

Ḥadīth 9

عَنْ أَبِي هُرَيْرَةَ رضي الله عنه، قَالَ: خَرَجَ رَسُولُ اللهِ ﷺ ذَاتَ يَوْمٍ - أَوْ قال: لَيْلَةٍ - فَإِذَا هُوَ بِأَبِي بَكْرٍ وَعُمَرَ، فَقَالَ: مَا أَخْرَجَكُمَا مِنْ بُيُوتِكُمَا هَذِهِ السَّاعَةَ؟ قَالَا: الْجُوعُ يَا رَسُولَ اللهِ، قَالَ: وَأَنَا، وَالَّذِي نَفْسِي بِيَدِهِ، لَأَخْرَجَنِي الَّذِي أَخْرَجَكُمَا، قُومُوا، فَقَامُوا مَعَهُ، فَأَتَى رَجُلًا مِنَ الْأَنْصَارِ فَإِذَا هُوَ لَيْسَ فِي بَيْتِهِ، فَلَمَّا رَأَتْهُ الْمَرْأَةُ، قَالَتْ: مَرْحَبًا وَأَهْلًا، فَقَالَ لَهَا رَسُولُ اللهِ ﷺ: أَيْنَ فُلَانٌ؟ قَالَتْ: ذَهَبَ يَسْتَعْذِبُ لَنَا مِنَ الْمَاءِ، إِذْ جَاءَ الْأَنْصَارِيُّ، فَنَظَرَ إِلَى رَسُولِ اللهِ ﷺ وَصَاحِبَيْهِ، ثُمَّ قَالَ: الْحَمْدُ لِلَّهِ مَا أَحَدٌ الْيَوْمَ أَكْرَمَ أَضْيَافًا مِنِّي، قَالَ: فَانْطَلَقَ، فَجَاءَهُمْ بِعِذْقٍ فِيهِ بُسْرٌ وَتَمْرٌ وَرُطَبٌ، فَقَالَ: كُلُوا مِنْ هَذِهِ، وَأَخَذَ الْمُدْيَةَ، فَقَالَ لَهُ رَسُولُ اللهِ ﷺ: إِيَّاكَ، وَالْحَلُوبَ، فَذَبَحَ لَهُمْ، فَأَكَلُوا مِنَ الشَّاةِ

وَمِنْ ذَلِكَ الْعِذْقِ وَشَرِبُوا، فَلَمَّا أَنْ شَبِعُوا وَرَوُوا، قَالَ رَسُولُ اللهِ ﷺ لِأَبِي بَكْرٍ، وَعُمَرَ: وَالَّذِي نَفْسِي بِيَدِهِ، لَتُسْأَلُنَّ عَنْ هَذَا النَّعِيمِ يَوْمَ الْقِيَامَةِ، أَخْرَجَكُمْ مِنْ بُيُوتِكُمُ الْجُوعُ، ثُمَّ لَمْ تَرْجِعُوا حَتَّى أَصَابَكُمْ هَذَا النَّعِيمُ.

(رواه مسلم)

Abū Hurayra ﷺ narrates:

One day the Messenger of Allah ﷺ went out and unexpectedly found Abū Bakr and ʿUmar ﷺ. He asked, "What brought the two of you out of your homes at this hour?" They replied, "Hunger, O Messenger of Allah." He said, "I swear by Him in Whose Hands is my life, I was brought out by the same thing that brought you out. Come with me." They went to [the house of] a man from the Anṣār, but at that time he was not home. However, when the woman of the house saw them, she said, "Welcome!" The Messenger of Allah ﷺ asked her, "Where is so-and-so?"[10] She replied, "He went to get fresh water for us."

---

10 Referring to the man of the house.

When the Anṣārī man arrived, he saw the Messenger of Allah ﷺ and his two Companions and said, "All praise be to Allah! On this day, there is no one with more honorable guests than me." He then stepped away and brought back a branch that had on it a variety of ripe, dried, and fresh dates. He said, "Eat from this," as he grabbed a large knife [to slaughter an animal for his guests]. The Messenger of Allah ﷺ said to him, "Do not slaughter a milk-bearing animal." So, the Anṣārī man slaughtered a sheep for them. They ate from the roasted sheep and dates and drank until they satisfied their hunger and quenched their thirst. Then the Messenger of Allah ﷺ said to Abū Bakr and ʿUmar, "I swear by Him in Whose Hands is my life, you will most definitely be questioned about this great blessing on the Day of Resurrection. Hunger expelled you from your homes and you did not return until you were bestowed with this blessing."

(Muslim)

Commentary

There are many beautiful aspects of this ḥadīth. First of all, the Best of Creation, the Chosen Messenger ﷺ was compelled to leave his home out of sheer hunger, seeking the grace of his Lord. It is worth pausing to reflect on the state in which Allah ﷻ kept His most beloved slave.

The Ḥadīth Master, Ḥāfiẓ ʿAbd al-Raʾūf al-Munāwī, mentions a subtle point, "The Prophet ﷺ did not come out of his home to ask for food or to seek someone for this purpose. The status of the Prophet ﷺ was too great for him to wander door-to-door, asking for food. Rather, he came out seeking the bounty of his Lord, and the bounty of his Lord sought out the Beloved."

Next, we see the two Companions, Abū Bakr and ʿUmar ﵄—who to this day are laid to rest next to the Messenger of Allah ﷺ—were going through the same condition as their beloved. Those who are the closest to the Messenger ﷺ are the ones whose internal and external states resemble his the most. These two honorable souls chose the same state of asceticism and abstinence from worldly pleasures that their beloved, the Messenger of Allah ﷺ chose and they were ultimately joined with him.

Finally, the ḥadīth shows the extent of reckoning we will all face on the Day of Judgment; even the elect who were faced with severe hunger will be questioned about the food they ate and the bounties they were bestowed. What then could be said about us, who hardly see any days of hunger and hardship, yet bask in Allah's bounties on a daily basis? We ask Allah for ease and well-being in this life and the next.

STRUGGLES
DURING THE CHILDHOOD OF THE
BELOVED PROPHET

صلى الله عليه واله وسلم

ما رآه ﷺ من المشقّة في صغره

Some of the Hardships and Difficulties He ﷺ Experienced In His Childhood

ذِكْرُ وَفَاةِ عَبْدِ اللهِ أَبِيهِ ﷺ

عَنِ ابْنِ شِهَابٍ، قَالَ: بَعَثَ عَبْدُ الْمُطَّلِبِ عَبْدَ اللهِ بْنَ عَبْدِ الْمُطَّلِبِ يَمْتَارُ لَهُ تَمْرًا مِنْ يَثْرِبَ، فَتُوُفِّيَ عَبْدُ اللهِ بْنُ عَبْدِ الْمُطَّلِبِ، ووَلَدَتْ آمِنَةُ رَسُولَ اللهِ ﷺ، ابْنَ عَبْدِ اللهِ، فَكَانَ فِي حِجْرِ جَدِّهِ عَبْدِ الْمُطَّلِبِ.

(رواه عبد الرزّاق)

H A D Ī T H (10)

عَنْ مُحَمَّدِ بْنِ إِسْحَاقَ بْنِ يَسَارٍ، قَالَ: وَقَدْ هَلَكَ أَبُوهُ عَبْدُ اللهِ وَهِيَ حُبْلَى ...

(دلائل النبوّة للإمام البيهقي)

H A D Ī T H (11)

The Death of His Father, ʿAbdullah ibn ʿAbd al-Muṭṭalib

Ibn Shihāb narrates

ʿAbd al-Muṭṭalib sent (his son) ʿAbdullah to gather dates from Yathrib. However, he passed away on the journey and Āmina gave birth to the Messenger of Allah ﷺ, the son of ʿAbdullah, after which he remained in the custody of his grandfather ʿAbd al-Muṭṭalib."

(ʿAbd al-Razzāq and Bayhaqī)

MUḤAMMAD IBN ISḤĀQ IBN YASĀR NARRATES:

The father of the Messenger of Allah ﷺ, ʿAbdullah, passed away while his mother was pregnant with him…

(Bayhaqī in *Dalāʾil al-Nubuwwah*)

وَفَاةُ أُمِّهِ آمِنَةَ بِنْتِ وَهْبٍ

ḤADĪTH 12

عَنْ مُحَمَّدِ بْنِ إِسْحَاقَ، قَالَ حَدَّثَنِي عَبْدُ اللهِ بْنُ أَبِي بَكْرِ بْنِ حَزْمٍ، قَالَ: قَدِمَتْ آمِنَةُ بِنْتُ وَهْبٍ أُمُّ رَسُولِ اللهِ ﷺ، عَلَى أَخْوَالِهِ مِنْ بَنِي عَدِيِّ بْنِ النَّجَّارِ، الْمَدِينَةَ، ثُمَّ رَجَعَتْ بِهِ حَتَّى إِذَا كَانَتْ بِالْأَبْوَاءِ هَلَكَتْ بِهَا، وَرَسُولُ اللهِ ﷺ، ابْنُ سِتِّ سِنِينَ.

(دلائل النبوّة للامام البيهقي)

The Death of His Mother, Āmina bint Wahb

Muḥammad ibn Isḥāq narrates that ʿAbdullah ibn Abū Bakr ibn Ḥazm said to him:

> Āmina bint Wahb, the mother of the Messenger of Allah ﷺ, came to Madīnah to visit some of his maternal uncles who were from the tribe of Banu ʿAdī ibn Najjār. When she was returning from the journey she passed away in a place called Abwāʾ. At that time the Messenger of Allah ﷺ was six years old.

(Bayhaqī in *Dalāʾil al-Nubuwwah*)

Ḥadīth 13

وَفَاةِ جَدِّهِ عَبْدِ الْمُطَّلِبِ بْنِ هَاشِمٍ

حَدَّثَنَا يُونُسُ، عَنِ ابْنِ إِسْحَاقَ، قَالَ وَمَاتَ عَبْدُ الْمُطَّلِبِ وَالنَّبِيُّ ﷺ ابْنُ ثَمَانِ سِنِينَ، فَلَمْ يَبْكِ أَحَدٌ كَانَ قَبْلَهُ بُكَاءَهُ.

(دلائل النبوّة للامام البيهقي)

The Death of His Grandfather, ʿAbd al-Muṭṭalib ibn Hāshim

Yūnus narrates that Muḥammad ibn Isḥāq said:

> ʿAbd al-Muṭṭalib passed away when the Messenger of Allah ﷺ was eight years old and no one cried before him, the way he cried.

(Bayhaqī in *Dalāʾil al-Nubuwwah*)

Commentary

One's childhood is that period of life when a person is most impressionable, when emotions run deepest, and memories remain for a lifetime. The ḥadīths in this chapter show the losses suffered by the Messenger of Allah ﷺ during such a sensitive time. The loss of one's parents and guardian can never be made up for by someone else, no matter how much love they show. However, the life of the Messenger of Allah ﷺ was unique in that Allah took it upon Himself to nurture the Leader of all mankind. He was destined to fulfill a great task and carry a colossal burden on his shoulders, and none but Allah Himself could prepare him for it.

As Allah ﷻ mentions in the Qur'ān:

﴿وَوَجَدَكَ ضَالًّا فَهَدَىٰ﴾

"We found you unaware, and then We guided you."

(Qur'ān 93:7)

And He ﷻ says:

﴿وَكَذَٰلِكَ أَوْحَيْنَا إِلَيْكَ رُوحًا مِّنْ أَمْرِنَا ۚ مَا كُنتَ تَدْرِي مَا الْكِتَابُ
وَلَا الْإِيمَانُ وَلَٰكِن جَعَلْنَاهُ نُورًا نَّهْدِي بِهِ مَن نَّشَاءُ مِنْ عِبَادِنَا ۚ وَإِنَّكَ
لَتَهْدِي إِلَىٰ صِرَاطٍ مُّسْتَقِيمٍ﴾

"So, we have revealed a spirit to you by Our command. You did not know what was the Book or what was faith, however, We made it a light that guides whomever We will from amongst Our slaves. And you definitely give guidance to a straight path."

(Qur'ān 42: 52)

Furthermore, in a narration of Ibn Ḥibbān and Bazzār, the Messenger of Allah ﷺ mentioned:

مَا هَمَمْتُ بِشَيْءٍ مِمَّا كَانَ أَهْلُ الْجَاهِلِيَّةِ يَعْمَلُوْنَ بِهِ غَيْرَ مَرَّتَيْنِ كُلُّ ذَلِكَ يَحُوْلُ اللهُ بَيْنِي وَبَيْنَ مَا أُرِيْدُ مِنْ ذَلِكَ ثُمَّ مَا هَمَمْتُ بَعْدَهَا بِشَيْءٍ حَتَّى أَكْرَمَنِيَ اللهُ بِرِسَالَتِهِ

(رواه بزار وابن حبان. قال الهيثمي في المجمع: رجاله ثقات)

"[Prior to prophethood,] I never considered doing anything from the actions of the people of *jāhiliyyah*,[11] except on two occasions. In both instances, Allah obstructed me from what I had intended. After that, I never considered any such notion ever again, until eventually Allah honored me with His Message (i.e. revelation)."

A narration of Bayhaqī elaborates that this incident occurred during the youth of the Prophet ﷺ, when he used to work as a shepherd. One night he headed towards a place that would be frequented by the youth. Before he could reach his destination, Allah caused a deep slumber to overcome him, and he did not awaken until the rising of the sun the next morning. This repeated itself on a subsequent night, after which he never entertained such thoughts ever again.

Even before the Messenger of Allah ﷺ was bestowed with revelation and granted the mantle of Prophethood, it was Allah Himself who was guiding the Prophet, directing him to the truth, and guarding him from evil.

---

11 The ignorant actions of the idolators of Makkah.

شق صدره الشريف لزيادة الكرامة، وليتلقى ما يوحى إليه

The Opening of His Chest to Prepare Him for the Divine Revelation That He Was to Receive

Ḥadīth 14

عَنْ أَنَسِ بْنِ مَالِكٍ ﷺ أَنَّ رَسُولَ اللهِ ﷺ أَتَاهُ جِبْرِيلُ - صَلَّى اللهُ عَلَيْهِ وَسَلَّمَ - وَهُوَ يَلْعَبُ مَعَ الْغِلْمَانِ، فَأَخَذَهُ فَصَرَعَهُ، فَشَقَّ عَنْ قَلْبِهِ، فَاسْتَخْرَجَ الْقَلْبَ، فَاسْتَخْرَجَ مِنْهُ عَلَقَةً، فَقَالَ: هَذَا حَظُّ الشَّيْطَانِ مِنْكَ، ثُمَّ غَسَلَهُ فِي طَسْتٍ مِنْ ذَهَبٍ بِمَاءِ زَمْزَمَ، ثُمَّ لَأَمَهُ، ثُمَّ أَعَادَهُ فِي مَكَانِهِ، وَجَاءَ الْغِلْمَانُ يَسْعَوْنَ إِلَى أُمِّهِ - يَعْنِي ظِئْرَهُ - فَقَالُوا: إِنَّ مُحَمَّدًا قَدْ قُتِلَ، فَاسْتَقْبَلُوهُ وَهُوَ مُنْتَقِعُ اللَّوْنِ، قَالَ أَنَسٌ: وَقَدْ كُنْتُ أَرَى أَثَرَ ذَلِكَ الْمِخْيَطِ فِي صَدْرِهِ

(رواه مسلم)

Anas ibn Mālik ﷺ narrates:

Jibrīl, peace and blessings of Allah be upon him, came to the Messenger of Allah ﷺ (in his childhood) while

> he was playing with some other children. He took hold of him, laid him on the ground, opened his chest, removed his heart, and extracted a blood-clot from it. He then mentioned, "This is the portion for Shayṭān [had it remained within you.]"[12] He then washed his heart with the water of Zamzam in a golden basin, mended it, and returned it to its place.
>
> The boys came running to his [foster] mother[13] and said, "Muḥammad has been killed!" They all rushed toward him [and found him alright]. However, his complexion was pale. Anas says, "I, myself, saw the marks of stitches on his chest."

(Muslim)

Commentary

In *al-Mawāhib al-Laduniyya*, Imām al-Qasṭallānī ﵀ quotes Imām Subkī ﵀ as saying:

> This blood-clot being referred to as the "portion of Shayṭān" was created in the noble entity of the Messenger because it is something that all humans are born with. Allah created

[12] Meaning this would prevent any impulsive thoughts from reaching him, and cutoff the attempts of Shayṭān in making him unmindful. (*Mirqāt al-Mafātīḥ Sharḥ Mishkāt al-Maṣābīḥ*)

[13] His wet-nurse

him with it to complete his physical creation as a regular human being, which was essential. However, the removal of this portion came about later by divine order.

This was to establish his lofty status and superiority above all people. In essence, he ﷺ was a human, but not like any other human. Just like a diamond is a stone, but not like any other stone.

A hadith narrated in *Saḥīḥ Muslim* shows that the Messenger of Allah ﷺ shared these similarities with ordinary people; in that he was created by Allah with the potential to experience all that normal people experience in the unseen realm—*with the clear difference* that Allah preserved him from being affected by any evil, sin, or whispering of devils.

ʿAbdullah ibn Masʿūd رضي الله عنه narrates that the Messenger of Allah ﷺ said, "There is none of you except that a companion from amongst the jinn is appointed to him." The people asked, "And you have one as well, O Messenger of Allah?" He replied, "And I as well. Except that Allah has granted me power over him, thus it does not call me to anything but good."

We see here that he ﷺ also had a jinn appointed to him, just like every other person. However as a manifestation of the Messenger's lofty status and his being divinely protected from all evil, a being whose nature is to cause mischief and deviation was transformed into an entity of goodness due to its close attachement to the Messenger of Allah ﷺ.

HIS SACRIFICES IN CALLING TO THE WAY OF ALLAH

صلى الله عليه وآله وسلم

مجاهدته ﷺ في تَحَمُّل المَشَاقّ لله تعالى

His ﷺ Struggles in Bearing Difficulties for the Sake of Allah

Ḥadīth 15

عَنْ أَنَسِ بْنِ مَالِكٍ رضي الله عنه قَالَ، قَالَ رَسُوْلُ اللهِ ﷺ: لَقَدْ أُخِفْتُ فِي اللهِ وَمَا يُخَافُ أَحَدٌ، وَلَقَدْ أُوْذِيْتُ فِي اللهِ وَمَا يُؤْذَى أَحَدٌ، وَلَقَدْ أَتَتْ عَلَيَّ ثَلَاثُوْنَ مِنْ بَيْنِ يَوْمٍ وَلَيْلَةٍ وَمَا لِي وَلِبِلَالٍ طَعَامٌ يَأْكُلُهُ ذُوْ كَبِدٍ إِلَّا شَيْءٌ يُوَارِيْهِ إِبْطُ بِلَالٍ.

(رواه الترمذي وقال هذا حديث حسن صحيح)

Anas ibn Mālik رضي الله عنه narrates:

The Messenger of Allah ﷺ said, "Verily, I have been threatened in the path of Allah like no other, and I have been harmed in the path of Allah like no other. Thirty days and nights would pass in which neither Bilāl nor I had anything that a living creature could eat, except a small portion that Bilāl would hide under his arm."

(Tirmidhī)

Commentary

This ḥadīth shows that the Messenger of Allah ﷺ was conveying the message of Allah in the early days of prophethood in the most dire circumstances. Despite his minimal support and lack of resources, with total reliance upon his Lord and perseverance, he eventually possessed the keys to the treasures of the world.

Mullā ʿAlī Qārī writes:

> In this utterance, the Prophet ﷺ is simply relating his condition and not complaining about the states he had to endure. He is proclaiming Allah's bounty upon him for enabling him to have patience upon the trials that were a means of attaining divine favor, and were the demand of divine love. It is also a consolation for the Ummah to help them tolerate any of the hardships that they may experience.[14]

[14] *Jamʿ al-Wasāʾil*

شدّة تلقّي الوحي

The Severity of Receiving Divine Revelation

Ḥadīth 16

عَنْ عَائِشَةَ، أُمِّ المُؤْمِنِينَ ﵂، أَنَّ الحَارِثَ بْنَ هِشَامٍ ﵁ سَأَلَ رَسُولَ اللهِ ﷺ فَقَالَ: يَا رَسُولَ اللهِ، كَيْفَ يَأْتِيكَ الوَحْيُ؟ فَقَالَ رَسُولُ اللهِ ﷺ: أَحْيَانًا يَأْتِينِي مِثْلَ صَلْصَلَةِ الجَرَسِ، وَهُوَ أَشَدُّهُ عَلَيَّ، فَيُفْصَمُ عَنِّي وَقَدْ وَعَيْتُ عَنْهُ مَا قَالَ، وَأَحْيَانًا يَتَمَثَّلُ لِي المَلَكُ رَجُلًا فَيُكَلِّمُنِي فَأَعِي مَا يَقُولُ. قَالَتْ عَائِشَةُ: ﵂ وَلَقَدْ رَأَيْتُهُ يَنْزِلُ عَلَيْهِ الوَحْيُ فِي اليَوْمِ الشَّدِيدِ البَرْدِ، فَيَفْصِمُ عَنْهُ وَإِنَّ جَبِينَهُ لَيَتَفَصَّدُ عَرَقًا.

(رواه البخاري)

ʿĀʾisha, the Mother of the Believers, ﵂ narrates:

Ḥārith ibn Hishām ﵁ asked, "O Messenger of Allah! How is revelation revealed to you?" Allah's Messenger

ﷺ replied, "Sometimes it is [revealed] like the ringing of a bell—this form of revelation is the hardest of all—and then this state passes after I have grasped what is inspired. Sometimes the Angel comes in the form of a man and talks to me and I grasp whatever he says." ʿĀʾisha added, "I saw revelation come down to the Prophet on a very cold day, and noticed the sweat dripping from his forehead [from the weight of the revelation]."

(Bukhārī)

مجاهدته ﷺ عند تلقي الوحي وبدء النبوة

His ﷺ Struggles When Receiving Revelation and at the Beginning of Prophethood

Ḥadīth 17

عَنْ عَائِشَةَ رضي الله عنها قالت : كَانَ أَوَّلُ مَا بُدِئَ بِهِ رَسُولُ اللهِ ﷺ مِنَ الْوَحْيِ الرُّؤْيَا الصَّادِقَةَ فِي النَّوْمِ، فَكَانَ لَا يَرَى رُؤْيَا إِلَّا جَاءَتْ مِثْلَ فَلَقِ الصُّبْحِ، ثُمَّ حُبِّبَ إِلَيْهِ الْخَلَاءُ، فَكَانَ يَخْلُو بِغَارِ حِرَاءٍ يَتَحَنَّثُ فِيهِ - وَهُوَ التَّعَبُّدُ - اللَّيَالِيَ أُوْلَاتِ الْعَدَدِ، قَبْلَ أَنْ يَرْجِعَ إِلَى أَهْلِهِ وَيَتَزَوَّدُ لِذَلِكَ، ثُمَّ يَرْجِعُ إِلَى خَدِيجَةَ فَيَتَزَوَّدُ لِمِثْلِهَا، حَتَّى فَجِئَهُ الْحَقُّ وَهُوَ فِي غَارِ حِرَاءٍ ...

ʿĀʾisha رضي الله عنها narrates,

Among the first signs of revelation for the Messenger of Allah ﷺ were true dreams. He would not see any dream except that it would come to pass as clear as the light of dawn. Then solitude started becoming beloved to him, so he would frequent the Cave of Ḥirāʾ, worshipping therein with fervor, spending many a night there before returning to his family. He would prepare provisions for this, and [after they would finish] he would return to Khadīja, similarly prepare provisions [and return again]. This went on until the Truth became manifest to him while he was in the Cave of Ḥirāʾ…

...فَجَاءَهُ الْمَلَكُ، فَقَالَ: اقْرَأْ، قَالَ: مَا أَنَا بِقَارِئٍ، قَالَ: فَأَخَذَنِي، فَغَطَّنِي حَتَّى بَلَغَ مِنِّي الْجَهْدَ، ثُمَّ أَرْسَلَنِي، فَقَالَ: اقْرَأْ، قَالَ: قُلْتُ: مَا أَنَا بِقَارِئٍ. قَالَ: فَأَخَذَنِي، فَغَطَّنِي الثَّانِيَةَ حَتَّى بَلَغَ مِنِّي الْجَهْدَ، ثُمَّ أَرْسَلَنِي، فَقَالَ: أَقْرَأْ، فَقُلْتُ: مَا أَنَا بِقَارِئٍ، فَأَخَذَنِي، فَغَطَّنِي الثَّالِثَةَ حَتَّى بَلَغَ مِنِّي الْجَهْدَ، ثُمَّ أَرْسَلَنِي، فَقَالَ:

﴿ٱقْرَأْ بِٱسْمِ رَبِّكَ ٱلَّذِى خَلَقَ ۞ خَلَقَ ٱلْإِنسَـٰنَ مِنْ عَلَقٍ ۞ ٱقْرَأْ وَرَبُّكَ ٱلْأَكْرَمُ ۞ ٱلَّذِى عَلَّمَ بِٱلْقَلَمِ ۞ عَلَّمَ ٱلْإِنسَـٰنَ مَا لَمْ يَعْلَمْ﴾

…An angel came to him and said, "Read!" The Messenger of Allah ﷺ said, "I cannot read!" [The Messenger of Allah ﷺ continues,] "Then the angel seized me, and gripped me so tight that I could bear it no further, then he released me and said again, 'Read!' I replied, 'I cannot read!' The angel seized me once again, and gripped me so tight that I could bear it no further, then he released me [again] and said, 'Read!' I responded, 'I cannot read!' The angel then seized me a third time and gripped me so tight that I could bear it no further, then he released me and said:

> "*Read in the name of your Lord who created. Created man from a clot. Read, and your Lord is the most Generous. The One Who taught by the pen. Taught man that which he knew not.*"[15]

... فَرَجَعَ بِهَا رَسُولُ اللهِ ﷺ تَرْجُفُ بَوَادِرُهُ، حَتَّى دَخَلَ عَلَى خَدِيجَةَ، فَقَالَ: زَمِّلُونِي زَمِّلُونِي، فَزَمَّلُوهُ حَتَّى ذَهَبَ عَنْهُ الرَّوْعُ، ثُمَّ قَالَ لِخَدِيجَةَ: أَيْ خَدِيجَةُ، مَا لِي؟ وَأَخْبَرَهَا الْخَبَرَ، قَالَ: لَقَدْ خَشِيتُ عَلَى نَفْسِي، قَالَتْ لَهُ خَدِيجَةُ: كَلَّا أَبْشِرْ، فَوَاللهِ، لَا يُخْزِيكَ اللهُ أَبَدًا، وَاللهِ، إِنَّكَ لَتَصِلُ الرَّحِمَ، وَتَصْدُقُ الْحَدِيثَ،

15 Qur'ān 96:1–5

وَتَحْمِلُ الْكَلَّ، وَتُكْسِبُ الْمَعْدُومَ، وَتَقْرِي الضَّيْفَ، وَتُعِينُ عَلَى نَوَائِبِ الْحَقِّ...

[…After this was over,] the Messenger of Allah ﷺ returned with these verses, trembling. He came to Khadīja saying, "Cover me, cover me!" She covered him until his fear abated. He said to Khadīja, "O Khadīja, what is happening to me?" Thereupon he relayed the story to her and said, "I fear for myself!" Khadīja said, "Never! Glad tidings be to you! I swear by Allah that Allah shall never disgrace you! By Allah, you join ties of kinship, you speak only truth, you bear the loads of others, you give to the destitute, you are hospitable to guests, and you relieve those who are suffering!"…

... فَانْطَلَقَتْ بِهِ خَدِيجَةُ حَتَّى أَتَتْ بِهِ وَرَقَةَ بْنَ نَوْفَلِ بْنِ أَسَدِ بْنِ عَبْدِ الْعُزَّى، وَهُوَ ابْنُ عَمِّ خَدِيجَةَ أَخِي أَبِيهَا، وَكَانَ امْرَأً تَنَصَّرَ فِي الْجَاهِلِيَّةِ، وَكَانَ يَكْتُبُ الْكِتَابَ الْعَرَبِيَّ، وَيَكْتُبُ مِنَ الْإِنْجِيلِ بِالْعَرَبِيَّةِ مَا شَاءَ اللهُ أَنْ يَكْتُبَ، وَكَانَ شَيْخًا كَبِيرًا قَدْ عَمِيَ، فَقَالَتْ

لَهُ خَدِيجَةُ: أَيْ عَمِّ، اسْمَعْ مِنَ ابْنِ أَخِيكَ، قَالَ وَرَقَةُ بْنُ نَوْفَلٍ: يَا ابْنَ أَخِي، مَاذَا تَرَى؟ فَأَخْبَرَهُ رَسُولُ اللهِ ﷺ خَبَرَ مَا رَآهُ، فَقَالَ لَهُ وَرَقَةُ: هَذَا النَّامُوسُ الَّذِي أُنْزِلَ عَلَى مُوسَى - صَلَّى اللهُ عَلَيْهِ وَسَلَّمَ، يَا لَيْتَنِي فِيهَا جَذَعًا، يَا لَيْتَنِي أَكُونُ حَيًّا حِينَ يُخْرِجُكَ قَوْمُكَ، قَالَ رَسُولُ اللهِ ﷺ: أَوَ مُخْرِجِيَّ هُمْ؟ قَالَ وَرَقَةُ: نَعَمْ لَمْ يَأْتِ رَجُلٌ قَطُّ بِمَا جِئْتَ بِهِ إِلَّا عُودِيَ، وَإِنْ يُدْرِكْنِي يَوْمُكَ أَنْصُرْكَ نَصْرًا مُؤَزَّرًا ".

(رواه البخاري ومسلم واللفظ له)

وزاد البخاري: ثُمَّ لَمْ يَنْشَبْ وَرَقَةُ أَنْ تُوُفِّيَ، وَفَتَرَ الوَحْيُ فَتْرَةً، حَتَّى حَزِنَ رَسُولُ اللهِ ﷺ.

...Khadīja then took the Messenger of Allah to Waraqa ibn Nawfal, who was the cousin of Khadīja ﵂ [Waraqa] had converted to Christianity during the [pre-Islamic] times of ignorance. He would transcribe the Injīl (Gospel) into Arabic, and he had finished transcribing as much as Allah had allowed for him to transcribe. He was a very elderly man who had gone blind.

Khadīja said to him, "O uncle, listen to your nephew!"[16] So Waraqa said, "O my nephew, what do you have to say?" The Prophet ﷺ informed him of what he saw. Waraqa then said, "This is the same bearer of good news (Jibrīl ﷺ), who was sent to Mūsā, peace and blessings of Allah be upon him. If only I was still youthful and strong! If only I could be alive when your people expel you [from your city]..." The Messenger of Allah ﷺ asked, "Will they really expel me?" Waraqa replied, "Yes. No man has brought what you have brought (i.e. revelation), except that he has been persecuted. If I happen to be alive at that time, I will surely assist you." [However, it was not long before Waraqa passed away, and the divine revelation [temporarily] ceased, causing the Messenger of Allah ﷺ to grieve deeply.][17]

(Bukhārī and Muslim)

Commentary

The entire mission of the Prophet ﷺ was full of difficulty, but the very beginning of revelation was particularly difficult. Initially, the Prophet ﷺ spent long periods of time secluded

16 According to the tradition of the Arabs, someone who is significantly older is affectionately referred to as an "uncle" and someone significantly younger as a "nephew."

17 Additional point mentioned in the narration of Bukhārī.

in the Cave of Ḥirā'. Then, in his first encounter with the angel, Jibrīl ﷺ, each embrace utterly drained the Messenger of Allah ﷺ physically; nevermind what the spiritual weight of receiving *waḥī* (revelation) might have been like. What the Messenger of Allah ﷺ experienced was so taxing that upon returning home he was trembling out of anxious fear. Next, Waraqa ibn Nawfal informs him, "No man has come with what you have come with, except that he has been persecuted." In other words, he ﷺ is being informed that enduring tribulation is part and parcel of being a prophet, and that there is more hardship to come.

We see that the Prophet ﷺ is experiencing various emotional states throughout this ḥadīth: his desire for solitude before *waḥī*, fear immediately after the start of *waḥī*, and severe grief—out of yearning for the Divine proximity—when revelation stops for some time. These are the various effects of the intense spiritual power of *waḥī*, which we simply cannot fathom.

Some people reject this ḥadīth on the grounds that it indicates the Prophet ﷺ felt fear and anxiety, and that this is not befitting for the prophets. However, the great Ḥadīth Master, Qāḍī ʿIyāḍ has a section on this in his *Shifā*, in which he states that every physical and emotional state that can overcome a normal human being can come upon a prophet as well. The difference, however, is that Allah has protected the prophets from those mental, physical, emotional, and spiritual states that are defects or deficiencies.

He gives the example of Mūsā ﷺ who, upon seeing his staff turn into a snake, was so frightened that he turned around and ran without looking back. Fear, anxiety, hope, and even sadness can be experienced by prophets. The sensation of such emotions are not deficiencies. Rather, they are absolutely normal. The issue is not whether they experience them or not, as they are but human; rather, the issue is recognizing and understanding what their response was. And the response of the Prophet ﷺ, throughout the difficulties of his life, was *istiqāmah*—firm resilience and steadfast recourse to Allah.

The bottom line will always be: along the path, there will always be challenges and hardship. In order for a person to come closer to Allah, Allah tests that person. Hardships and tests are a sign that Allah loves someone. He simply wants to see how much we love Him and how much are we willing to endure for His sake.

مجاهدته ﷺ في تبليغ الرسالة وما لَقِيَهُ مِنْ قَوْمِهِ

The Struggle of the Prophet ﷺ in Delivering the Message and the Backlash He Faced from His People

Ḥadīth 18

عَنِ ابْنِ عَبَّاسٍ رضي الله عنهما قَالَ: لَمَّا نَزَلَتْ ﴿وَأَنْذِرْ عَشِيرَتَكَ الأَقْرَبِينَ﴾ صَعِدَ النَّبِيُّ ﷺ عَلَى الصَّفَا، فَجَعَلَ يُنَادِي: يَا بَنِي فِهْرٍ، يَا بَنِي عَدِيٍّ - لِبُطُونِ قُرَيْشٍ - حَتَّى اجْتَمَعُوا فَجَعَلَ الرَّجُلُ إِذَا لَمْ يَسْتَطِعْ أَنْ يَخْرُجَ أَرْسَلَ رَسُولاً لِيَنْظُرَ مَا هُوَ، فَجَاءَ أَبُو لَهَبٍ وَقُرَيْشٌ، فَقَالَ: أَرَأَيْتَكُمْ لَوْ أَخْبَرْتُكُمْ أَنَّ خَيْلاً بِالوَادِي تُرِيدُ أَنْ تُغِيرَ عَلَيْكُمْ، أَكُنْتُمْ مُصَدِّقِيَّ؟ قَالُوا: نَعَمْ، مَا جَرَّبْنَا عَلَيْكَ إِلَّا صِدْقًا، قَالَ: فَإِنِّي نَذِيرٌ لَكُمْ بَيْنَ يَدَيْ عَذَابٍ شَدِيدٍ. فَقَالَ أَبُو لَهَبٍ: تَبًّا لَكَ سَائِرَ اليَوْمِ، أَلِهَذَا جَمَعْتَنَا؟ فَنَزَلَتْ: ﴿تَبَّتْ يَدَا أَبِي لَهَبٍ وَتَبَّ مَا أَغْنَى عَنْهُ مَالُهُ وَمَا كَسَبَ﴾

(رواه البخاري)

Ibn ʿAbbās ؓ narrates:

When the verse "And warn your closest kinsmen…"[18] was revealed, the Prophet ﷺ climbed Mt. Ṣafā and began to call out, "O Tribe of Fihr! O Tribe of ʿAdiy!"—intending by it the people of Quraysh—until the people gathered. If a man was unable to come out himself [to hear what was being said], he sent someone on his behalf to see what it was about. Abū Lahab came, as did the Quraysh. The Prophet ﷺ said, "Tell me, if I were to inform you that an army is in the valley [leading to Makkah] intending to invade you, would you believe me?" They responded, "Yes, we have never experienced from you [anything] but the truth." He ﷺ replied, "Then, I [have come to you] as a warner of a severe punishment that is before you." [Hearing this,] Abū Lahab said, "May evil befall you forever! Is this why you have gathered us?"

Thereafter, the verses, "May the two hands of Abū Lahab perish, and may he perish. His wealth and what he earned did not avail him…"[19] were revealed.

(Bukhārī)

---

18 Qurʾān 26:214

19 Qurʾān 111:1-2

Commentary

In a lengthier version of this ḥadīth, narrated in *Ṣaḥīḥ Muslim*, the Messenger of Allah ﷺ actually calls out to the Quraysh by mentioning the names in their shared lineage—reminding them of the close ties of kinship that exist between them, "O progeny of Kaʿb ibn Luʿay, save yourselves from the Fire! O progeny of Murra ibn Kaʿb, save yourselves from the Fire! O progeny of ʿAbd al-Shams, save yourselves from the Fire! O progeny of ʿAbd Manāf, save yourselves from the Fire! O progeny of Hāshim, save yourselves from the fire! O progeny of ʿAbd al-Muṭṭalib, save yourselves from the Fire! O Fāṭima, save yourself from the Fire! For verily I cannot help you [escape from the punishment] of Allah, except for the ties of kinship which I will continue to maintain."

This incident is probably one of the first instances in which the Messenger of Allah ﷺ openly invites his tribe and kin to Islam. We get a sense of the sincerity, fervor and emotion with which the Prophet ﷺ admonished his people; for he knew that if they did not shun idolatry and oppression, they would be overtaken by the wrath of Allah. His deep concern and worry for them overflows from his blessed words and heartfelt entreaties.

This crucial moment can be looked at from many perspectives, but the main point we wish to highlight is the abandonment and rejection that the Prophet faced from his own kith and kin. If we are misunderstood and rejected by total strangers, it is not as painful as being rejected and abandoned by our own family. Prior to this incident, the Prophet ﷺ was held in high honor and esteemed by his people; yet no sooner than he conveyed the truth, for the sake of their own salvation, did they revile him and begin to persecute and torture him. Imagine trying to save a close relative or friend from falling into a raging fire or a deep pit; in return that person curses you and begins to torture you—how disturbing and shocking would that be? What the Prophet experienced from his own relatives was worse than this. Despite that, he continued to honor their ties of kinship and call his people to Allah with heartfelt concern.

In this moment, wherein the Prophet ﷺ was calling his people to salvation, his own uncle—the brother of his father—screams out the most foul insults and makes the crowd disperse and scatter.

After this, the Messenger of Allah ﷺ returned to his home with great sadness and grief. It caused such pain to the Prophet ﷺ that Allah revealed Sūrah al-Masad, in its entirety, as a curse upon Abū Lahab and his treacherous wife. Abū Lahab—whose real name was ʿAbd al-ʿUzza ibn ʿAbd al-Muṭṭalib—was an uncle of the Messenger of Allah ﷺ and one of the staunchest opponents of the Prophetic message. He would actively dissuade people from paying any heed to his nephew, the Messenger of Allah ﷺ, and his wife, Umm Jamīl, would join him in readily harassing the Prophet ﷺ despite their close familial ties.

This incident shows us that some of the worst torment faced by the Messenger of Allah ﷺ was from his tribesmen and members of his own family. Hence, Allah ﷻ consoled his beloved to remain steadfast, exercise patience, and remember his Lord through prayer and remembrance:

﴿وَلَقَدْ نَعْلَمُ أَنَّكَ يَضِيقُ صَدْرُكَ بِمَا يَقُولُونَ ۝ فَسَبِّحْ بِحَمْدِ رَبِّكَ وَكُن مِّنَ السَّاجِدِينَ ۝ وَاعْبُدْ رَبَّكَ حَتَّىٰ يَأْتِيَكَ الْيَقِينُ﴾

We do indeed know how your heart is distressed at what they say. So, glorify the praises of your Lord, and be of those who prostrate themselves in adoration; and worship your Lord until certainty (death) comes to you.

(Qur'ān 15:97-99)

The revelation of Sūrah al-Masad also demonstrates that those who hurl curses and behave insolently with the prophets and people of Allah will themselves be cursed and reviled by Allah. Those who spend their wealth and energies against the cause of Islam will ultimately fail and wallow in regret.

HADĪTH 19

عَنْ جُبَيْرِ بْنِ نُفَيْرٍ قَالَ: جَلَسْنَا إِلَى الْمِقْدَادِ بْنِ الْأَسْوَدِ يَوْمًا، فَمَرَّ بِهِ رَجُلٌ، فَقَالَ: طُوبَى لِهَاتَيْنِ الْعَيْنَيْنِ اللَّتَيْنِ رَأَتَا رَسُولَ اللهِ ﷺ، وَاللهِ لَوَدِدْنَا أَنَّا رَأَيْنَا مَا رَأَيْتَ، وَشَهِدْنَا مَا شَهِدْتَ، فَاسْتُغْضِبَ، فَجَعَلْتُ أَعْجَبُ، مَا قَالَ إِلَّا خَيْرًا، ثُمَّ أَقْبَلَ إِلَيْهِ، فَقَالَ: مَا يَحْمِلُ الرَّجُلَ عَلَى أَنْ يَتَمَنَّى مُحْضَرًا غَيَّبَهُ اللهُ عَنْهُ، لَا يَدْرِي لَوْ شَهِدَهُ كَيْفَ كَانَ يَكُونُ فِيهِ؟ وَاللهِ، لَقَدْ حَضَرَ رَسُولَ اللهِ ﷺ، أَقْوَامٌ أَكَبَّهُمُ اللهُ عَلَى مَنَاخِرِهِمْ فِي جَهَنَّمَ لَمْ يُجِيبُوهُ، وَلَمْ يُصَدِّقُوهُ، أَوَلَا تَحْمَدُونَ اللهَ، إِذْ أَخْرَجَكُمْ تَعْرِفُونَ رَبَّكُمْ، مُصَدِّقِينَ لِمَا جَاءَ بِهِ نَبِيُّكُمْ ﷺ، قَدْ كُفِيتُمُ الْبَلَاءَ بِغَيْرِكُمْ؟ وَاللهِ، لَقَدْ بُعِثَ النَّبِيُّ ﷺ عَلَى أَشَدِّ حَالٍ بُعِثَ عَلَيْهَا نَبِيٌّ مِنَ الْأَنْبِيَاءِ، وَفَتْرَةٍ وَجَاهِلِيَّةٍ مَا يَرَوْنَ أَنَّ دِينًا أَفْضَلُ مِنْ عِبَادَةِ الْأَوْثَانِ، فَجَاءَ بِفُرْقَانٍ فَرَّقَ بَيْنَ الْحَقِّ وَالْبَاطِلِ، وَفَرَّقَ بَيْنَ الْوَالِدِ وَوَلَدِهِ، حَتَّى إِنْ كَانَ الرَّجُلُ لَيَرَى وَلَدَهُ أَوْ وَالِدَهُ أَوْ أَخَاهُ كَافِرًا، وَقَدْ فَتَحَ اللهُ قُفْلَ قَلْبِهِ لِلْإِيمَانِ، يَعْلَمُ أَنَّهُ إِنْ هَلَكَ دَخَلَ النَّارَ، فَلَا تَقَرُّ عَيْنُهُ وَهُوَ يَعْلَمُ أَنَّ حَبِيبَهُ فِي النَّارِ، وَأَنَّهَا الَّتِي قَالَ اللهُ: ﴿الَّذِينَ يَقُولُونَ رَبَّنَا هَبْ لَنَا مِنْ أَزْوَاجِنَا وَذُرِّيَّاتِنَا قُرَّةَ أَعْيُنٍ...﴾ الْآيَة

(رواه ابن حبان في صحيحه)

Jubayr ibn Nufayr narrates:

> We were sitting with Miqdād ibn al-Aswad ﵁ one day when a man passed by and said, "How blessed are those eyes which saw the Messenger of Allah ﷺ! By Allah, we would have loved to see what you have seen and witness what you have witnessed!" [Miqdād ﵁] was angered by this, and I was surprised because the man had only said good. He turned to him and said, "What is it that makes a man wish to have lived during an era that Allah has prevented him from witnessing? Whereas he does not even know how his situation would have been therein! By Allah, there were people who were present in the time of the Messenger of Allah ﷺ whom Allah threw headlong into the Hellfire [because] they neither answered his call nor believed in him. Will you then not thank Allah for bringing you to believe in your Lord, bearing witness to the truth that your Prophet ﷺ came with, while the hardship and struggles were borne by others? By Allah, the Prophet ﷺ was sent in the midst of the harshest conditions that any prophet was sent in, during an era without any prophet and in [a time of] ignorance in which the people saw no religion better than the worship of idols. Then he brought the Criterion (the Qurʾān), which distinguished the truth from falsehood, and separated between father and son; such that a man would see his son, father, or brother in a state of disbelief—while Allah had opened up his

heart to belief—knowing that if they were to die [in this state] they would enter the Fire. Thus, his heart would not be contented knowing that his loved one is in the Fire. And this is what is referred to in the verse:

[And] those who say, 'O Our Lord! Grant us from amongst our spouses and our progeny the coolness of our eyes.'"[20]

(Ibn Ḥibbān)

Commentary

In this ḥadīth, a *tābiʿī*—someone who lived an entire generation after the Prophet's time and never witnessed the difficulties of that era—is expressing his love for the Prophet ﷺ to one of the Ṣaḥābah.[21] The response of the Ṣaḥābī[22] surprised the narrator. The contrast between the spirit of the *tābiʿī's* statement and that of the Ṣaḥābī's reaction reveals an insight that only a Ṣaḥābī could have: the intensity of the trials they faced out of their love for the Messenger ﷺ. They struggled and sacrificed in ways that no one else could truly understand.

---

20 Qurʾān 25:74

21 The Companions of the Prophet, who lived in his era, believed in him, and died with faith.

22 Singular for Ṣaḥābah.

He reminds the *tābiʿī* that he should be grateful for whatever state Allah has placed him in, for he does not know if he would have been able to handle the intensity of trial that came with being amongst the first generation of believers.

This ḥadīth also puts into sharp perspective the nature of our difficulties compared to that which the first believers had to endure. Miqdād ﵁ is informing us that we should be grateful for having Islam in the era and circumstances that we do because if we were subjected to the kinds of trials and tribulations the people before us underwent, we do not know what our outcome would be (implying that we would not be able to handle it). Thus, we should be thankful for the comforts that Allah blesses us with, as well as the relative ease of the trials we undergo.

HADĪTH 20

عَنْ الْحَارِثُ بْنُ الْحَارِثِ الْغَامِدِيُّ ﵁، قَالَ: قُلْتُ لِأَبِي: مَا هَذِهِ الْجَمَاعَةُ؟ قَالَ: هَؤُلَاءِ الْقَوْمُ قَدِ اجْتَمَعُوا عَلَى صَابِئٍ لَهُمْ، قَالَ: فَنَزَلْنَا فَإِذَا رَسُولُ اللهِ ﷺ يَدْعُو النَّاسَ إِلَى تَوْحِيدِ اللهِ عَزَّ وَجَلَّ وَالْإِيمَانِ بِهِ، وَهُمْ يَرُدُّونَ عَلَيْهِ وَيُؤْذُونَهُ، حَتَّى انْتَصَفَ

النَّهَارُ وَانْصَدَعَ عَنْهُ النَّاسُ، وَأَقْبَلَتِ امْرَأَةٌ قَدْ بَدَا نَحْرُهَا تَحْمِلُ قَدَحًا وَمِنْدِيلًا، فَتَنَاوَلَهُ مِنْهَا وَشَرِبَ وَتَوَضَّأَ، ثُمَّ رَفَعَ رَأْسَهُ وَقَالَ: يَا بُنَيَّةُ خَمِّرِي عَلَيْكِ نَحْرَكِ، وَلَا تَخَافِي عَلَى أَبِيكِ. قُلْنَا: مَنْ هَذِهِ؟ قَالُوا: زَيْنَبُ بِنْتُهُ.

(رواه الطبراني في الكبير وقال الهيثمي: رجاله ثقات)

ḤĀRITH IBN AL-ḤĀRITH ﷺ NARRATES:

I asked my father, "Who are these people gathered together?" He replied, "They are a group that have banded with a heretic from amongst them."[23] Then we approached and [saw] the Messenger of Allah ﷺ calling people to believe in one God, Allah, and to have faith in Him. They were rebuking and tormenting him until midday, at which point the people left him. A woman, whose neck had become exposed, approached carrying a container of water and a cloth. [The Prophet] ﷺ took them from her, drank, and performed the ritual ablution. Then, he ﷺ lifted his head and said, "O my beloved daughter, cover up your neck, and do not fear

23 The narrator is mentioning an incident he observed in childhood, before becoming a Muslim.

for your father." We asked, "Who was that [woman]?" They replied, "She was Zaynab, his daughter."

(Ṭabarānī)

ḤADĪTH 21

عن أشعث عن رجل من كنانة قال: رَأَيْتُ رَسُولَ اللهِ ﷺ بِسُوقِ ذِي الْمَجَازِ يَتَخَلَّلُهَا يَقُولُ: يَا أَيُّهَا النَّاسُ، قُولُوا لَا إِلَهَ إِلَّا اللهُ تُفْلِحُوا. قَالَ: وَأَبُو جَهْلٍ يَحْثِي عَلَيْهِ التُّرَابَ وَيَقُولُ: يَا أَيُّهَا النَّاسُ، لَا يَغُرَّنَّكُمْ هَذَا عَنْ دِينِكُمْ، فَإِنَّمَا يُرِيدُ لِتَتْرُكُوا آلِهَتَكُمْ، وَتَتْرُكُوا اللَّاتَ وَالْعُزَّى...

(رواه أحمد و قال الهيثمي: رجاله رجال الصحيح)

ASHʿATH [IBN SULAYM] NARRATES FROM A MAN FROM THE TRIBE OF KINĀNA, WHO SAID:

I saw the Prophet ﷺ going through the marketplace of Dhu 'l-Majāz (in Makkah) saying, "Proclaim [that]

'There is no one worthy of worship except Allah' and you will prosper!" At the same time, Abū Jahl[24] [was behind him] throwing dust upon him and saying, "Do not let this man mislead you from your religion; for he only wishes to deviate you from worshipping your gods and from worshipping Lāt and ʿUzza!"

(Aḥmad)

HADĪTH 22

عَنْ اِبْنِ عَبَّاس ﵄ فِيْ قِصَّةٍ طَوِيْلَةٍ جَرَتْ بَيْنَ الْمُشْرِكِيْنَ وَبَيْنَ
النَّبِيِّ ﷺ، فَلَمَّا قَامَ عَنْهُمْ رَسُولُ اللهِ ﷺ قَالَ أَبُو جَهْلٍ: يَا مَعْشَرَ
قُرَيْشٍ، إِنَّ مُحَمَّدًا قَدْ أَبَى إِلَّا مَا تَرَوْنَ مِنْ عَيْبِ دِيْنِنَا، وَشَتْمِ

---

[24] Abū Jahl, ʿAmr ibn Hishām ibn al-Mughīra, was one of fiercest enemies of Islam. Known to the idolators of Makkah by the agnomen Abū 'l-Ḥakam, he was given the title Abū Jahl—the Father of Ignorance—by the Messenger of Allah ﷺ due to his knowing no-limit in his brutal persecution of the Muslims. His torment and tyranny reached the point that upon his death in the battle of Badr, the Prophet ﷺ referred to him as "the *Firʿawn* (Pharoah) of this Ummah."

آبَائِنَا، وَتَسْفِيهِ أَحْلَامِنَا، وَشَتْمِ آلِهَتِنَا، وَإِنِّي أُعَاهِدُ اللهَ لَأَجْلِسَنَّ لَهُ غَدًا بِحَجَرٍ مَا أُطِيقُ حَمْلَهُ. فَإِذَا سَجَدَ فِي صَلَاتِهِ فَضَخْتُ بِهِ رَأْسَهُ فَأَسْلِمُونِي عِنْدَ ذَلِكَ أَوِ امْنَعُونِي، فَلْيَصْنَعْ بَعْدَ ذَلِكَ بَنُو عَبْدِ مَنَافٍ مَا بَدَا لَهُمْ. قَالُوا: وَاللهِ لَا نُسْلِمُكَ لِشَيْءٍ أَبَدًا، فَامْضِ لِمَا تُرِيدُ...

IBN ʿABBĀS ﷺ NARRATES IN A LONG INCIDENT REGARDING A PLOT MADE BY THE IDOLATORS AGAINST THE PROPHET ﷺ:

> When [the Messenger of Allah ﷺ] departed from them, Abū Jahl said, "O people of Quraysh! Indeed, Muḥammad is adamant about cursing our religion, disgracing our forefathers, belittling our ideology, and insulting our idols. I swear by Allah,[25] I will ambush him tomorrow with a [large] rock. When he goes into prostration, I will crush his skull. After that, let the clan of ʿAbd Manāf[26] do about it whatever they want...."

---

25 The idolators of Makkah believed in Allah. However, they ascribed partners unto Him.

26 The name of the clan of the Prophet ﷺ. He was from the sub-clan of Hāshim which was part of the larger clan of ʿAbd Manāf. With this statement, Abū Jahl was taunting the Prophet's clan.

...فَلَمّا أَصْبَحَ أَبُو جَهْلٍ، أَخَذَ حَجَرًا كَمَا وَصَفَ ثُمّ جَلَسَ لِرَسُولِ اللهِ ﷺ يَنْتَظِرُهُ. وَغَدَا رَسُولُ اللهِ ﷺ كَمَا يَغْدُو، وَكَانَ بِمَكّةَ وَقِبْلَتُهُ إلَى الشّامِ، فَكَانَ إذَا صَلّى صَلّى بَيْنَ الرُّكْنَيْنِ: الرّكْنِ الْيَمَانِيّ وَالْأَسْوَدِ، وَجَعَلَ الْكَعْبَةَ بَيْنَهُ وَبَيْنَ الشّامِ. فَقَامَ يُصَلّي وَقَدْ غَدَتْ قُرَيْشٌ، فَجَلَسُوا فِي أَنْدِيَتِهِمْ يَنْتَظِرُونَ مَا أَبُو جَهْلٍ فَاعِلٌ. فَلَمّا سَجَدَ رَسُولُ اللهِ ﷺ احْتَمَلَ أَبُو جَهْلٍ الْحَجَرَ، ثُمّ أَقْبَلَ نَحْوَهُ حَتّى إذَا دَنَا مِنْهُ رَجَعَ مُنْهَزِمًا, مُنْتَقَعًا لَوْنُهُ مَرْعُوبًا. قَدْ يَبِسَتْ يَدَاهُ عَلَى حَجَرِهِ. حَتّى قَذَفَ الْحَجَرَ مِنْ يَدِهِ. وَقَامَتْ إلَيْهِ رِجَالُ قُرَيْشٍ. فَقَالُوا لَهُ مَا لَك يَا أَبَا الْحَكَمِ؟ قَالَ قُمْت إلَيْهِ لِأَفْعَلَ بِهِ مَا قُلْت لَكُمْ الْبَارِحَةَ فَلَمّا دَنَوْتُ مِنْهُ عَرَضَ لِي دُونَهُ فَحْلٌ مِنْ الْإِبِلِ لَا وَاَللهِ مَا رَأَيْت مِثْلَ هَامَتِهِ وَلَا مِثْلَ قَصَرَتِهِ وَلَا أَنْيَابِهِ لِفَحْلِ قَطّ. فَهَمّ بِي أَنْ يَأْكُلَنِي.

(رواه ابن هشام في سيرته وأورده الذهبي في سير أعلام النبلاء)

...So in the morning, Abū Jahl took a large rock and waited in ambush. The Prophet ﷺ came and began to pray between the two corners [of the Kaʿbah], the Black

Stone and the Yemeni Corner, [because his habit was] he would pray in the direction of Shām.[27] Meanwhile, the Quraysh were gathering in their [usual] meeting place. When the Messenger of Allah ﷺ prostrated, Abū Jahl lifted the rock and walked towards him. But once he drew near, he [suddenly] retreated, frightened, his face drained of all color. His hands turned stiff, due to which he dropped the rock. Some of the men from the Quraysh got up and asked, "What is wrong with you, O Abū 'l-Ḥakam?"[28] He replied, "I went to him, to do what I told you. But when I drew near, a menacing camel blocked me from reaching him. I swear by Allah, I have never seen the likes of its head, neck, or teeth—and it was about to devour me."[29]

(Ibn Hishām and *Siyar al-Aʿlām al-Nubalā'*)

[27] The name for the Levant or Greater Syria, which was the first *qiblah* (direction of prayer) for the Muslims.

[28] The original nickname that the Quraysh had for Abū Jahl.

[29] Allah made Abū Jahl perceive a terrifying camel-like creature standing guard over the Prophet ﷺ as he prayed.

HADĪTH 23

عَنْ أَبِي هُرَيْرَةَ رضي الله عنه قَالَ: قَالَ أَبُو جَهْلٍ: هَلْ يُعَفِّرُ مُحَمَّدٌ وَجْهَهُ بَيْنَ أَظْهُرِكُمْ؟ قَالَ: فَقِيلَ: نَعَمْ، فَقَالَ: وَاللَّاتِ وَالْعُزَّى! لَئِنْ رَأَيْتُهُ يَفْعَلُ ذَلِكَ لَأَطَأَنَّ عَلَى رَقَبَتِهِ، أَوْ لَأُعَفِّرَنَّ وَجْهَهُ فِي التُّرَابِ، قَالَ: فَأَتَى رَسُولَ اللَّهِ ﷺ وَهُوَ يُصَلِّي زَعَمَ لِيَطَأَ عَلَى رَقَبَتِهِ، قَالَ: فَمَا فَجِئَهُمْ مِنْهُ إِلَّا وَهُوَ يَنْكِصُ عَلَى عَقِبَيْهِ، وَيَتَّقِي بِيَدَيْهِ، قَالَ: فَقِيلَ لَهُ: مَا لَكَ؟ فَقَالَ: إِنَّ بَيْنِي وَبَيْنَهُ لَخَنْدَقًا مِنْ نَارٍ وَهَوْلًا وَأَجْنِحَةً، فَقَالَ رَسُولُ اللَّهِ ﷺ: لَوْ دَنَا مِنِّي لَاخْتَطَفَتْهُ الْمَلَائِكَةُ عُضْوًا عُضْوًا...

(رواه مسلم)

ABŪ HURAYRA رضي الله عنه NARRATES THAT:

Abū Jahl once asked, "Does Muḥammad have the audacity to rub his face in the dust in your midst?!"[30] Someone replied, "Yes." So, he said, "By Lāt and ʿUzza, if I saw him doing that, I would surely trample upon his neck or bury his face in the dirt!" So [when the Messenger of Allah ﷺ began praying,] he approached him as he was in prayer, intending to trample upon his neck. However, he abruptly turned back on his heels,

---

[30] Refering to the prostrations that the Prophet ﷺ would offer while in prayer.

protecting himself [from something unseen] with his hands. Someone asked him, "What is the matter with you?" He said, "Indeed, between me and him there is a trench of fire, terror, and wings [of angels]." The Messenger of Allah ﷺ then said, "Had he come just a little closer to me, the angels would have torn him apart, limb by limb."

(Muslim)

ḤADĪTH 24

عَن ابْنُ إِسْحَاق: وَحَدَّثَنِي يَعْقُوبُ بْنُ عُتْبَةَ بْنِ الْمُغِيرَةِ بْنِ الْأَخْنَسِ أَنَّهُ حُدِّثَ: أَنَّ قُرَيْشًا حِينَ قَالُوا لِأَبِي طَالِبٍ هَذِهِ الْمَقَالَةَ، بَعَثَ إِلَى رَسُولِ اللهِ ﷺ فَقَالَ لَهُ: يَا بْنَ أَخِي، إِنَّ قَوْمَكَ قَدْ جَاءُونِي، فَقَالُوا لِي كَذَا وَكَذَا - لِلَّذِي قَالُوا لَهُ - فَأَبْقِ عَلَيَّ وَعَلَى نَفْسِكَ، وَلَا تُحَمِّلْنِي مِنَ الْأَمْرِ مَا لَا أُطِيقُ. قَالَ: فَظَنَّ رَسُولُ اللهِ ﷺ أَنَّهُ قَدْ بَدَا لِعَمِّهِ فِيهِ بِدَاءٌ، وَأَنَّهُ خَاذِلُهُ وَمُسْلِمُهُ، وَأَنَّهُ قَدْ ضَعُفَ عَنْ نُصْرَتِهِ وَالْقِيَامِ مَعَهُ، قَالَ: فَقَالَ لَهُ رَسُولُ اللهِ ﷺ: يَا عَمِّ، وَاللهِ

لَوْ وَضَعُوا الشَّمْسَ فِي يَمِينِي، وَالْقَمَرَ فِي يَسَارِي، عَلَى أَنْ أَتْرُكَ هَذَا الْأَمْرَ حَتَّى يُظْهِرَهُ اللّٰهُ، أَوْ أَهْلِكَ فِيهِ، مَا تَرَكْتُهُ. قَالَ: ثُمَّ اسْتَعْبَرَ رَسُولُ اللّٰهِ ﷺ فَبَكَى، ثُمَّ قَامَ، فَلَمَّا وَلَّى نَادَاهُ أَبُو طَالِبٍ فَقَالَ: أَقْبِلْ يَا بْنَ أَخِي. فَأَقْبَلَ عَلَيْهِ رَسُولُ اللّٰهِ ﷺ فَقَالَ: اذْهَبْ يَا بْنَ أَخِي، فَقُلْ مَا أَحْبَبْتَ، فَوَاللّٰهِ لَا أُسْلِمُكَ لِشَيْءٍ أَبَدًا.

(رواه الذهبي في سير، وابن كثير في البداية، والبيهقي في دلائل النبوة)

Ibn Ishāq mentions that Ya'qūb ibn 'Utba ibn al-Mughīra ibn al-Akhnas narrated to him:

> The Quraysh once had a discussion with Abū Ṭālib[31] [after which] he sought out the Messenger of Allah ﷺ and said to him, "O my nephew! Indeed, your people have come to me, and sought from me such-and-such," referring to those things they had spoken to him about.

---

31 Abū Ṭālib ibn 'Abd al-Muṭṭalib was one of the chiefs of Quraysh, and the uncle of the Messenger of Allah ﷺ, who raised him like his own son after the passing of the Messenger's father, mother, and grandfather. He was very dear to Prophet ﷺ and the Prophet was very dear to him. Although he never embraced Islam, he remained a buffer against the Quraysh, guarding the Messenger of Allah ﷺ from their relentless persecution whenever he could. He passed away in the tenth year of Prophethood, three years before the Hijra.

"So spare me and yourself, and do not burden me with troubles that I cannot bear." The Messenger of Allah ﷺ thought that his uncle was considering abandoning him and turning him over [to his persecutors from the Quraysh], and that he had become too weak to support him and stand by his side. So, the Messenger of Allah ﷺ said to him, "O my uncle! By Allah, if they were to place the sun in my right hand and the moon in my left hand, I would not leave this effort—until Allah makes it dominant or I die in its cause." Tears flowed down the cheeks of the Messenger of Allah ﷺ and he stood up. But when he turned away, Abū Ṭālib called him back saying, "Come here." So, the Messenger of Allah ﷺ came back, and he [Abū Ṭālib] said, "Go on, my nephew, and preach as you wish, because, by Allah, I will never give you up for anything, ever."

(*Siyar al-Aʿlām al-Nubalāʾ*, *al-Bidāyah wal-Nihāyah*, and *Dalāʾil al-Nubuwwah* of al-Bayhaqī)

HADĪTH 25

عَنْ عَبْدِ اللهِ بْنِ جَعْفَرٍ رضي الله عنهما قَالَ: لَمَّا مَاتَ أَبُو طَالِبٍ عَرَضَ لِرَسُولِ اللهِ ﷺ سَفِيهٌ مِنْ قُرَيْشٍ، فَأَلْقَى عَلَيْهِ تُرَابًا، فَرَجَعَ إِلَى بَيْتِهِ، فَأَتَتْ بِنْتُهُ تمسح عن وجهه التراب وتبكي فجعل يَقُولُ: أَيْ بُنَيَّةَ لَا تَبْكِينَ، فَإِنَّ اللهَ مَانِعٌ أَبَاكِ ، وَيَقُولُ مَا بَيْنَ ذَلِكَ: مَا نَالَتْ مِنِّي قُرَيْشٌ شَيْئًا أَكْرَهُهُ حَتَّى مَاتَ أَبُو طَالِبٍ.

(رواه الذهبي في تاريخ الاسلام، والبيهقي في دلائل النبوة)

ʿAbdullah ibn Jaʾfar ﷺ narrates:

When Abū Ṭālib passed away, an insolent man from the Quraysh came before the Messenger of Allah ﷺ and threw dust upon him. So, he returned home and his daughter came, weeping, to wipe the dust from his face. He began [to console her] saying, "My beloved daughter, do not weep, because indeed Allah watches over and protects your father." Thereafter he mentioned, "The Quraysh did not succeed in doing anything reprehensible to me until Abū Ṭālib passed away."

(*Tārīkh al-Islām* of al-Dhahabī and *Dalāʾil al-Nubuwwah* of al-Bayhaqī)

H
A
D
Ī
T
H
(26)

عَنْ عُرْوَةَ بْنِ الزُّبَيْرِ، قَالَ: سَأَلْتُ عَبْدَ اللهِ بْنَ عَمْرٍو عَنْ أَشَدِّ مَا صَنَعَ الْمُشْرِكُونَ بِرَسُولِ اللهِ ﷺ. قَالَ: رَأَيْتُ عُقْبَةَ بْنَ أَبِي مُعَيْطٍ جَاءَ إِلَى النَّبِيِّ ﷺ وَهُوَ يُصَلِّي، فَوَضَعَ رِدَاءَهُ فِي عُنُقِهِ، فَخَنَقَهُ بِهِ خَنْقًا شَدِيدًا، فَجَاءَ أَبُو بَكْرٍ حَتَّى دَفَعَهُ عَنْهُ، فَقَالَ: أَتَقْتُلُونَ رَجُلًا أَنْ يَقُولَ رَبِّيَ اللهُ وَقَدْ جَاءَكُمْ بِالْبَيِّنَاتِ مِنْ رَبِّكُمْ؟

(رواه البخاري)

‘Urwa ibn Zubayr narrates:

I asked ‘Abdullah ibn ‘Umar 🙵 regarding the worst of what the idolaters did to the Messenger of Allah 🙵. He said, "I saw ‘Uqba ibn Abi Mu‘īṭ come to the Prophet 🙵 while he was praying. He put his shawl around the neck of the Prophet and began violently choking him with it. So, Abū Bakr 🙵 came, pushed him away from the Prophet and said, "Will you kill a man for saying, 'My Lord is Allah', whereas he has brought clear signs to you from your Lord?"

(Bukhārī)

ḤADĪTH 27

عَنْ عَبْدِ اللهِ رضي الله عنه، قَالَ: مَا رَأَيْتُ رَسُوْلَ اللهِ ﷺ دَعَا عَلَى قُرَيْشٍ
غَيْرَ يَوْمٍ وَاحِدٍ، فإِنَّهُ كَانَ يُصلِّيْ وَرَهْطٌ مِنْ قُرَيْشٍ جُلُوسٌ، وَسَلا
جَزُورٍ قَرِيبٌ مِنْهُ، فقَالُوْا: مَنْ يَأْخُذُ هذا السَّلاَ، فيُلْقِيَهِ عَلى
ظَهْرِهِ؟ قَالَ: فقَالَ عُقبةُ بْنُ أَبِيْ مُعَيْطٍ: أَنَا، فَأَخَذَهُ فَأَلْقَاهُ عَلى
ظَهْرِهِ، فلَمْ يَزَلْ سَاجِدًا، حَتّى جَاءَتْ فَاطِمَةُ صلواتُ اللهِ عليها،
فَأَخَذَتْهُ عَنْ ظَهْرِهِ، فقَالَ رَسُوْلُ اللهِ ﷺ: اللّهُمَّ عَلَيْكَ المَلأَ مِنْ
قُرَيْشٍ، اللّهمَّ عَلَيكَ بِعُتْبَةَ بْنِ رَبِيْعَةَ، اللّهُمَّ عَلَيْكَ بِشَيْبَةَ بْنِ رَبِيْعَةَ،
اللّهُمَّ عَلَيْكَ بِأَبِيْ جَهْلِ بْنِ هِشَامٍ، اللّهمَّ عَلَيْكَ بِعُقْبَةَ بْنِ أَبِيْ مُعَيْطٍ،
اللّهُمَّ عَلَيْكَ بِأُبَيِّ بْنِ خلَفٍ - أَوْ قَالَ: أُمَيَّةَ بْنِ خلَفٍ - قَالَ: قَالَ
عَبْدُ اللهِ: فَلَقَدْ رَأَيْتُهُمْ قُتِلُوا يَوْمَ بَدْرٍ جَمِيْعًا ...

(رواه أحمد)

ʿAbdullah ibn Masʿūd رضي الله عنه narrates that:

I did not see the Messenger of Allah ﷺ curse the Quraysh except once. The Prophet ﷺ was praying while a group of men from the Quraysh were sitting [near by], and the entrails of a slaughtered camel were in his vicinity. They asked, "Who will take these entrails and throw them on his back?" ʿUqba ibn Abī Muʿīt responded, "I will do it." So, he took them and threw them on the back of the Messenger of Allah ﷺ. He remained in prostration [in order to complete his prayer] until Fāṭima—may the blessings of Allah be upon her—came and removed them from his back. The Messenger of Allah ﷺ responded [to them, supplicating], "O Allah! Do away with the council of Quraysh. O Allah! Do away with ʿUtba ibn Rabīʿa. O Allah! Do away with Shayba ibn Rabīʿa. O Allah! Do away with Abū Jahl ibn Hishām. O Allah! Do away with ʿUqba ibn Abī Muʿīt. O Allah! Do away with Ubayy ibn Khalaf" or [the narrator said,] "Umayya ibn Khalaf."

ʿAbdullah [ibn Masʿūd continued] saying:

"Verily, I witnessed every single one of them killed on the day of Badr ..."

(Aḥmad)

Commentary

The numerous ḥadīths on this topic highlight the same essential points: the difficulty the Prophet ﷺ underwent in spreading Islam, his steadfastness in the face of this difficulty, and the amazing ways in which Allah ﷻ protected him. This protection sometimes manifested through miracles, like the images that Abū Jahl was shown; or through moral support, as in the example of Abū Ṭālib; or in Allah answering his duʿāʾ in a very direct and apparent manner, such as the last ḥadīth mentioned above.

It should be noted, however, that the Messenger of Allah ﷺ never experienced difficulties without being given inspirational support directly from Allah ﷻ. This came in the form of Qurʾānic revelation, showing him that all prophets endured such difficulties. In the same way, the Ṣaḥābah were also reminded by Allah about the people who came before them, who also underwent intense difficulty on the path of Allah (such as the Aṣḥāb al-Ukhdūd).[32]

Taking this into consideration, we should not reflect on the trials and difficulties of the Prophet ﷺ and his Companions simply to develop an unhealthy sense of guilt. Rather, remembering their sacrifices strengthens us by reminding us that we belong to a people and a community of believers who lived and thrived in trials and tribulations. Hence, we realize that faith and *dīn* grow and are established through hardship, whereas they are weakened and slip away in the face of luxury and comfort. Lastly, we learn that if we remain steadfast and put our full trust in Allah, we will find Him to be the Greatest Support and Caretaker.

---

[32] The Aṣḥāb al-Ukhdūd, or "People of the Trench", are mentioned in Sūrah al-Burūj. They were believers from one of the previous nations that were burnt alive in trenches of fire for believing in Allah alone as their Lord and Creator.

مقاطعة قريش لرسول الله ﷺ و قبيلته و المسلمين

The Boycott of the Quraysh Against the Messenger Of Allah ﷺ, His Clan, and the Muslims

Ḥadīth 28

عَنْ أَبِي هُرَيْرَةَ رضي الله عنه قَالَ: قَالَ لَنَا رَسُوْلُ اللهِ ﷺ، وَنَحْنُ بِمِنًى: نَحْنُ نازِلُونَ غَدًا بِخَيفِ بَنِي كِنَانَةِ، حَيْثُ تَقَاسَمُوْا عَلَى الكُفْرِ، وَذٰلِكَ أَنَّ قُرَيْشًا وَبَنِي كِنَانَةَ حَالَفَتْ عَلَى بَنِي هاشِمٍ وَبَنِي المُطَّلِبِ؛ أَنْ لَا يُنَاكِحُوْهُمْ، وَلَا يبَايِعُوْهُم، حَتّى يُسْلِموا إِلَيْهِمْ رَسُوْلَ اللهِ ﷺ. يَعْنِيْ بِذلِكَ: المُحصَّب.

(رواه البخاري و مسلم)

Abū Hurayra رضي الله عنه narrates:

The Messenger of Allah ﷺ said to us while we were in Mina, "We will be descending into the Valley of Banū Kināna, the place where the idolaters took an oath of *kufr*."[33] And that was an alliance amongst the Quraysh and the tribe of Kināna formed against the clans of Hāshim and al-Muṭṭalib[34]—that they would not marry from them, nor conduct any business dealings with them, until they handed over the Messenger of Allah ﷺ to them." He meant by that [the place known as] al-Muḥaṣṣab.

(Bukhārī and Muslim)

Commentary

Imagine having a traumatic experience at a certain place, then passing by that same location many years later. How would you feel and what would you say?

This ḥadīth illustrates the recollection of trauma and oppression that the Prophet ﷺ experienced in his early days in Makkah. He is sharing what he went through in that dismal situation many years ago with his Companions. He is relating to them the history of that location—a reminder of the helplessness, incapacity, and near-defeat of his Ummah; compared to their current state—heading towards triumph, victory, and domination. He does this to uplift the hearts of his Companions so that they may be grateful for Allah's

33 Disbelief

34 The clans of the Prophet ﷺ.

bounty and assistance. And to remind them that verily with difficulty comes ease.

Ibn Isḥāq relates that this boycott and exile took place during the month of Muḥarram in the seventh year of Prophethood and lasted three years. They were confined to the outskirts of Makkah, in a valley known as the Valley of Abū Ṭālib or Banu Kinānah. This cruel and barbaric boycott of the Prophet's ﷺ tribe was an ultimatum from the Quraysh, to force them to give up Islam and turn the Prophet ﷺ over to them.

The Quraysh made a pact that banned all interaction with Banu Hāshim, whether in marriage, trade, or by aiding them in any way with food or provisions. These sanctions were so severe that the crying of the children could be heard from the other side of the valley. Having been reduced to eating the leaves of trees and bushes due to the scarcity of food, their stool resembled the droppings of goats. The cruelty reached such an extent that even some of the non-believers from the Quraysh wanted it to come to an end.

ʿAllāma Suhaylī narrates an incident in *Al-Rawḍ al-Unuf* about Saʿd ibn Abī Waqqāṣ ؓ who tells of his story during that harsh time:

> "I came out one night to relieve myself when I heard a crackling under my feet. When I looked to see what it was, it turned out to be a dry piece of camel skin.

> So I took it and washed it, then I roasted it in the fire, grinded it to pieces, mixed it with water and drank it. It gave me strength for three days."

Abū Jahl would approach foreign traders who would come to Makkah for business and say to them:

> "O traders! Inflate your rates and prices upon Muḥammad and his Companions so that they are unable to buy anything from you! Verily, you know me and you know how I fulfill my promises. I guarantee that you will not see any loss! Double the price of your commodities so that he goes back empty handed to his children [while] they are wailing out of hunger!"

So the traders would return to Abū Jahl after denying the Prophet ﷺ and his Companions a fair deal and he would pay them double. The believers were left in utter destitution and unimaginable suffering as a result of this ruthlessness.

Nevertheless, this inhumane boycott would ultimately end through a miraculous event. The oppressive pact was recorded on parchment and stored in the Kaʿbah for safe keeping. In it, all the injustices that were to be committed against the Prophet ﷺ and his followers were recorded along with the names of the leaders of the Quraysh who had agreed to it.

Allah had ordered termites to eat away at this parchment until nothing remained of it except the name of Allah that was written at the top. The Prophet ﷺ was informed by Jibrīl ﷺ that all of the injustices that were recorded had been done away with. The Prophet ﷺ asked his uncle to convey this message to the Quraysh.

When Abū Ṭālib went to the Quraysh, he said, "Verily, my nephew has conveyed to me that the pact has been done away with, so bring your document and if it is as he says then put an end to this brutality of yours; and if it is not true, then I will turn him over to you." They agreed upon this and took an oath upon it. They brought their parchment and saw it was exactly as the Messenger of Allah ﷺ had said. This infuriated them even more and prompted them to increase their evil plans and further their schemes. However, a sympathetic group from amongst the Quraysh stood up and brought an end to their plot once and for all.[35]

As a direct result of the boycott, both Khadīja ﷺ and Abū Ṭālib soon passed away. It was an incredibly trying time for the Prophet ﷺ and his loyal Companions, but they endured with great resilience.

After reading the summary of these three years, imagine how it must have been to have seen it and to have lived it. This was what he was reminding his Companions about as he passed by that location.

---

35 *Al-Rawḍ al-Unuf*

Despite all that he experienced in this traumatic event, when the Prophet ﷺ triumphantly marched into Makkah many years later, with an army of ten thousand men, he forgave all of the people of Quraysh—even those who were responsible for inflicting so much personal loss upon him ﷺ and his family.

We ask Allah to bless our beloved Messenger ﷺ, his revered family and honorable Companions ﷺ and grant them eternal peace. And may He inspire us to endure our trials and tribulations with resilience, patience, and gratitude. *Āmīn.*

مجاهدته ﷺ عند القتال في سبيل الله تعالى

The Striving of the Prophet ﷺ During Expeditions in the Path of Allah the Exalted

Ḥadīth 29

عَنْ أَبِي هُرَيْرَةَ رضي الله عنه قَالَ: قَالَ رَسُوْلُ اللهِ ﷺ: ...لَوْلَا أَنْ أَشُقَّ عَلَى أُمَّتِيْ مَا قَعَدْتُ خَلْفَ سَرِيَّةٍ، وَلَوَدِدْتُ أَنِّيْ أُقْتَلُ فِيْ سَبِيْلِ اللهِ، ثُمَّ أُحْيَا، ثُمَّ أُقْتَلُ، ثُمَّ أُحْيَا، ثُمَّ أُقْتَلُ.

(رواه البخاري)

Abū Hurayra رضي الله عنه narrates:

The Messenger of Allah ﷺ said, "...If it would not have become difficult upon my Ummah, I would not have stayed behind from any expedition. I would love to be martyred in the path of Allah, then brought back to life, then martyred, then brought back to life, then martyred."

(Bukhārī)

ḤADĪTH 30

عَنْ سَهْلِ بْنِ سَعْدٍ السَّاعِدِيِّ رضي الله عنه قَالَ: جُرِحَ وَجْهُ رَسُولِ اللهِ ﷺ، وَكُسِرَتْ رَبَاعِيَتُهُ، وَهُشِمَتِ الْبَيْضَةُ عَلَى رَأْسِهِ، فَكَانَتْ فَاطِمَةُ بِنْتُ رَسُولِ اللهِ ﷺ تَغْسِلُ الدَّمَ، وَكَانَ عَلِيُّ بْنُ أَبِي طَالِبٍ يَسْكُبُ عَلَيْهَا بِالْمِجَنِّ، فَلَمَّا رَأَتْ فَاطِمَةُ أَنَّ الْمَاءَ لَا يَزِيدُ الدَّمَ إِلَّا كَثْرَةً، أَخَذَتْ قِطْعَةَ حَصِيرٍ فَأَحْرَقَتْهُ حَتَّى صَارَ رَمَادًا، ثُمَّ أَلْصَقَتْهُ بِالْجُرْحِ، فَاسْتَمْسَكَ الدَّمُ.

(رواه مسلم)

SAHL IBN SAʿD AS-SĀʿIDĪ رضي الله عنه NARRATES:

[On the day of Uḥud,] the face of the Messenger of Allah ﷺ was wounded, one of his front teeth was broken, and his helmet was crushed upon his head. So Fāṭima رضي الله عنها, the daughter of the Messenger of Allah ﷺ washed off the blood while ʿAlī ibn Abū Ṭālib رضي الله عنه poured water from a vessel. When Fāṭima رضي الله عنها saw that the water only increased the bleeding, she took a piece from a [date-palm] mat and burned it until it turned to ashes. Then she applied the ashes over the wound, thus the bleeding ceased.

(Muslim)

Indeed the enemies have transgressed against us;
If they intend to attack us, we shall repel them"

(Bukhārī)

Commentary

This series of ḥadīths highlights a few instances wherein the Prophet ﷺ experienced hardships during the course of some of his military expeditions. From dirt covering his blessed chest during the rigors of preparing the ditch in the Battle of Khandaq to the deep wounds suffered on his blessed head and cheek during the Battle of Uḥud; we catch glimpses of the sacrifices our Beloved Messenger ﷺ had to endure for this Ummah so that they might be blessed with the bounty of *dīn*. Now, let us consider: what was his attitude through all of this, and what should our attitude be in the face of difficulty?

His attitude towards sacrifice is exemplified in the first ḥadīth. The Messenger of Allah ﷺ reveals his heart's true desire: to march out and partake in every single battle so that he may be martyred again and again for Allah's sake. This was the zeal he ﷺ carried within himself. However, outwardly he tempered his actions knowing he was the ultimate example for all to follow; and as the leader of the people, he needed to be present to fulfill the many responsibilities Allah had bestowed upon him.

We see through these sacrifices the perfection of his leadership; his heart was filled with passion for the sake of Allah, yet his actions were still perfectly balanced. This is the height of human perfection; and we have only come to know the reality of what perfection truly is due to the sacrifices and difficulties the Messenger of Allah ﷺ went through.

By reading this section, we come to know of the physical sacrifices that were made in order for this dīn to be established in our lives and in the world. Whether worldly or after-worldly, nothing can be achieved without effort. Allah ﷻ mentions:

﴿وَالَّذِينَ جَاهَدُوا فِينَا لَنَهْدِيَنَّهُمْ سُبُلَنَا﴾

And those who struggle in Our cause, surely We shall guide them in our ways.

(Qur'ān 29:69)

It is also important to draw a distinction between the noble armed struggle of the Prophet ﷺ versus the many false claims of jihād that countless people make in our day and age. The jihād of the Messenger of Allah ﷺ, his rightly guided Khulafā and noble companions was divinely guided by revelation for the purpose of establishing truth and justice in the land according to the decree of Allah.

We clearly see the manifestation of Allah's direct guidance in the matter when it was done in the light of divine revelation; such that soon after these conquests, peace and justice would spread and people would rush to embrace the faith wholeheartedly. The greatest demonstration of this was that those who fought so fiercely against the Prophet ﷺ were shortly thereafter so eager to give their lives in his defense. His armed struggle, along with the assistance of his illustrious companions dispelled tyranny, disbelief and oppression.

Juxtapose this to the deceptive cries of jihād made by many ignorant people today, who in reality spread nothing but falsehood and cause more hurt to the lives of innocent people than dispel oppression and tyranny. They are nothing more than selfish independent struggles, arbitrarily established by charlatans to further their own personal objectives. They are far removed from the light of revelation and guidance, and the proof of their darkness is the wanton bloodshed and increased oppression that they spread; ultimately driving people away from truth and guidance. May Allah save us and guide the uninformed to the truth.

His Suffering at the Hands of the Creation

صلى الله عليه وآله وسلم

تحمّله ﷺ أذى الشياطين

The Prophet ﷺ Enduring the Harms of the Shayāṭīn

Ḥadīth 33

عَنْ عَبْدِ الرَّحْمٰنِ بْنِ خَنْبَشٍ رضي الله عنه أَنَّهُ سُئِلَ: أَدْرَكْتَ رَسُولَ اللهِ ﷺ؟ قَالَ: نَعَمْ، قَالَ: قُلْتُ: كَيْفَ صَنَعَ رَسُولُ اللهِ ﷺ لَيْلَةَ كَادَتْهُ الشَّيَاطِينُ، فَقَالَ: إِنَّ الشَّيَاطِينَ تَحَدَّرَتْ تِلْكَ اللَّيْلَةَ عَلَى رَسُولِ اللهِ ﷺ مِنَ الْأَوْدِيَةِ، وَالشِّعَابِ، وَفِيهِمْ شَيْطَانٌ بِيَدِهِ شُعْلَةُ نَارٍ، يُرِيدُ أَنْ يَحْرِقَ بِهَا وَجْهَ رَسُولِ اللهِ ﷺ، فَهَبَطَ إِلَيْهِ جِبْرِيلُ، فَقَالَ: يَا مُحَمَّدُ قُلْ، قَالَ: مَا أَقُولُ؟ قَالَ: قُلْ: أَعُوذُ بِكَلِمَاتِ اللهِ التَّامَّةِ مِنْ شَرِّ مَا خَلَقَ، وَذَرَأَ وَبَرَأَ، وَمِنْ شَرِّ مَا يَنْزِلُ مِنَ السَّمَاءِ، وَمِنْ شَرِّ مَا يَعْرُجُ فِيهَا، وَمِنْ شَرِّ فِتَنِ اللَّيْلِ وَالنَّهَارِ، وَمِنْ شَرِّ كُلِّ طَارِقٍ إِلَّا طَارِقًا يَطْرُقُ بِخَيْرٍ، يَا رَحْمٰنُ ، قَالَ: فَطَفِئَتْ نَارُهُمْ، وَهَزَمَهُمُ اللهُ تَبَارَكَ وَتَعَالَى.

(رواه أحمد وأبو يعلى. قال الهيثمي رجال أحدِ إسنادَيْ أحمد و أبي يعلى رجال الصحيح)

ʿAbd al-Raḥmān ibn Khambash ؓ narrates that someone asked him:

> "Did you meet the Messenger of Allah ﷺ?" He replied, "Yes." The person then asked, "What did the Messenger of Allah ﷺ do on the night when the *shayāṭīn*[37] plotted against him?" He said, "That night, the *shayāṭīn* descended towards the Messenger of Allah ﷺ [coming down] from the valleys and canyons. Amongst them was a *shayṭān* that had a torch of fire in its hand. It intended to burn the face of the Messenger of Allah ﷺ with it. So, Jibrīl ؑ descended upon the Prophet and said, "O Muḥammad, say!" The Prophet ﷺ said, "What should I say?" Jibrīl ؑ replied, "Say, 'I seek refuge in the most perfect words of Allah from the evil of whatever He has created, produced, and originated; from the evil of whatever descends from the sky and the evil of whatever ascends to it; from the evil afflictions of the night and day; and from the evil of every visitor of the night that comes, except for the one that comes with good, O Most Merciful!" Then [ʿAbd al-Raḥmān] said, "The fire of the *shayāṭīn* was extinguished and Allah, the Exalted, defeated them."

(Aḥmad and Abū Yaʿlā)

---

37 Devils or evil jinns. Jinns are one of the unseen creations of Allah. They were created from fire, and have been given the free-will to choose between faith and disbelief, like mankind. Many verses of the Qurʾān make reference to them.

تحمّله ﷺ أذى الهوامّ

His ﷺ Enduring the Harm of Dangerous Creatures

Ḥadīth 34

عَنْ عَلِيٍّ رضي الله عنه، قَالَ: بَيْنَا رَسُولُ اللهِ ﷺ ذَاتَ لَيْلَةٍ يُصَلِّي فَوَضَعَ
يَدَهُ عَلَى الْأَرْضِ فَلَدَغَتْهُ عَقْرَبٌ فَتَنَاوَلَهَا رَسُولُ اللهِ ﷺ بِنَعْلِهِ
فَقَتَلَهَا، فَلَمَّا انْصَرَفَ قَالَ: لَعَنَ اللهُ الْعَقْرَبَ مَا تَدَعُ مُصَلِّيًا،
وَلَا غَيْرَهُ أَوْ نَبِيًّا أَو غَيْرَهُ، ثُمَّ دَعَا بِمِلْحٍ وَمَاءٍ فَجَعَلَهُ فِي إِنَاءٍ ثُمَّ جَعَلَ
يَصُبُّهُ عَلَى إِصْبَعِهِ حَيْثُ لَدَغَتْهُ وَيَمْسَحُهَا، وَيُعَوِّذُهَا بِالْمُعَوِّذَتَيْنِ.

(رواه البيهقي في شعب الإيمان)

ʿAlī ibn Abī Ṭālib رضي الله عنه narrates:

One night, as the Messenger of Allah ﷺ was praying, he placed his hand upon the ground and a scorpion stung him. So, the Messenger of Allah ﷺ struck it and killed it with his sandal. When he came out of his prayer he said, "May Allah curse the scorpion. It does not leave a person whether or not he be in prayer, or whether or not he is a prophet." Then he asked for some salt and water. He mixed them in a container, and he began to pour it over his finger where the scorpion had stung him. He wiped over it as he recited Sūrah al-Falaq and Sūrah al-Nās.

(*Shuʿab al-Īmān* of al-Bayhaqī)

COMMENTARY

One might think that the amount of struggle and difficulty the Prophet ﷺ went through at the hands of man was enough, without also having to suffer from the attacks of unseen beings (*shayāṭīn*) and venomous creatures, like scorpions. And yet, Allah chose to expose His beloved ﷺ to difficulties at the hands of all kinds of creation. This was to manifest the *bashariyyah*[38] of His beloved Prophet ﷺ; that despite his lofty status as a Messenger, he was still a human being. To achieve such greatness while simultaneously experiencing human life is the pinnacle of excellence.

The divine plan of sending down an exemplar to mankind would not be fulfilled by having an angel, or some other immortal and invincible being, descend from the heavens. For Allah to have sent an angel to humankind—one who feels no pain, no hunger, and experiences no hardship—would have

38 The humanness of the Prophet ﷺ.

been futile because the people would have said, "How can we follow one who shows no similarity to us?!"

Rather, a true example and role model must fulfill the criteria of being one amongst the masses. He should be someone who shares in all human vulnerabilities, and in the face of these struggles show patience, gratitude, steadfastness, resilience, and reliance upon Allah. This is the manifestation of true excellence.

Furthermore, just as each type of *ʿibādah* (worship—e.g. ṣalāh, recitation of Qurʾān, *dhikr*, *ṣadaqah*) carries its own light (*nūr*) and spiritual effulgence, enlightening the soul, so does each trial. The spiritual effect of performing different types of *ʿibādah* is that one's light will be perfected. Similarly, every type of trial carries its own quality, and by patiently bearing various trials and tribulations, one's light will also be perfected.

Through these various difficulties, Allah is manifesting the perfection of the Prophet ﷺ as His slave—the culmination of all spiritual light and internal perfection.

In summary, the pain and hardship the Prophet ﷺ went through was of every type that we can imagine: physical, emotional, mental, and spiritual. But we also see that in every single difficulty his recourse was to Allah ﷻ alone. The result was nothing short of constant elevation of his status till the day he was united with the Highest Companion.

تَعَاقُد قريش على قتله و توكّله على ربه و حفظ الله اِيّاه ﷺ

The Pact of the Quraysh to Kill Him, His Trust upon His Lord, and Allah's Protection of Him ﷺ

Ḥadīth 35

عَنْ سَعِيدِ بْنِ جُبَيْرٍ، عَنِ ابْنِ عَبَّاسٍ رضي الله عنهما: أَنَّ الْمَلَأَ، مِنْ قُرَيْشٍ اجْتَمَعُوا فِي الْحِجْرِ، فَتَعَاهَدُوا بِاللَّاتِ، وَالْعُزَّى، وَمَنَاةَ الثَّالِثَةِ الْأُخْرَى: لَوْ قَدْ رَأَيْنَا مُحَمَّدًا، قُمْنَا إِلَيْهِ قِيَامَ رَجُلٍ وَاحِدٍ، فَلَمْ نُفَارِقْهُ حَتَّى نَقْتُلَهُ، قَالَ: فَأَقْبَلَتْ فَاطِمَةُ تَبْكِي حَتَّى دَخَلَتْ عَلَى أَبِيهَا، فَقَالَتْ: هَؤُلَاءِ الْمَلَأُ مِنْ قَوْمِكَ فِي الْحِجْرِ، قَدْ تَعَاهَدُوا: أَنْ لَوْ قَدْ رَأَوْكَ قَامُوا إِلَيْكَ فَقَتَلُوكَ، فَلَيْسَ مِنْهُمْ رَجُلٌ إِلَّا قَدْ عَرَفَ نَصِيبَهُ مِنْ دَمِكَ، قَالَ: يَا بُنَيَّةُ أَدْنِي وَضُوءًا. فَتَوَضَّأَ، ثُمَّ دَخَلَ عَلَيْهِمُ الْمَسْجِدَ، فَلَمَّا رَأَوْهُ، قَالُوا: هُوَ هَذَا، هُوَ هَذَا. فَخَفَضُوا أَبْصَارَهُمْ، وَعُقِرُوا فِي مَجَالِسِهِمْ، فَلَمْ يَرْفَعُوا إِلَيْهِ أَبْصَارَهُمْ، وَلَمْ يَقُمْ مِنْهُمْ رَجُلٌ، فَأَقْبَلَ رَسُولُ اللهِ ﷺ حَتَّى قَامَ عَلَى رُءُوسِهِمْ، فَأَخَذَ

قَبْضَةً مِنْ تُرَابٍ، فَحَصَبَهُمْ بِهَا، وَقَالَ: شَاهَتِ الْوُجُوهُ. قَالَ: فَمَا

أَصَابَتْ رَجُلاً مِنْهُمْ حَصَاةٌ إِلَّا قُتِلَ يَوْمَ بَدْرٍ كَافِرًا

(رواه أحمد. قال الهيثمي: رواه أحمد بإسنادين ورجال أحدهما رجال الصحيح).

S aʿīd ibn Jubayr narrated from Ibn ʿAbbās 🌸 :

The leaders of Quraysh gathered in the Ḥijr[39] and took a covenant by Lāt, ʿUzza, Manāt the Third One:[40] "If we see Muḥammad we will all stand against him, as one body, and we will not leave him until we kill him." [Upon hearing this,] Fāṭima [the daughter of the Messenger 🌸] went forth crying until she came to her father and said, "The leaders of your people are in the Ḥijr. They have made a pact that if they see you, they will go after you and kill you! There isn't a single man amongst them, except that he has accepted a share in spilling your blood." [The Messenger of Allah 🌸] replied, "My Beloved Daughter, bring me some water for *wuḍūʾ* (ablution)." So he performed *wuḍūʾ* and then came to them in the masjid. When [the Quraysh] saw him, they said, "There he is! There he is!" However, their

---

[39] The Ḥijr is the immediate area on the northwest side of the Kaʿbah that is encompassed by a short circular wall. It, and the area within, is considered to be a portion of the Kaʿbah.

[40] These are the names of different idols that were worshipped by the Quraysh.

gazes were lowered and they were fixed to their places, unable to get up. They could not even raise their gaze towards him. Not a single man from amongst them could stand against him. So, the Messenger of Allah ﷺ approached [them], until he stood over their heads. He seized a handful of earth, and threw it at them saying, "May their faces be disfigured!" Every single man that was struck by one of those pebbles was killed on the day of Badr as a disbeliever.

(Aḥmad)

Commentary

This narration illustrates the ardent reliance and deep trust that the Prophet ﷺ had in his Lord. If one of us were to be informed that the authorities of our community or some local gangs have formed alliances to kill us, how would we react? It is only natural to panic and be overwhelmed with fear. However, we see an example of the Prophet's ﷺ connection with Allah, that even at this fearful juncture he is reassured by his trust in his Lord. This is similar to Prophet Hūd ﷺ who boldly told his people:

﴿قَالَ إِنِّيٓ أُشۡهِدُ ٱللَّهَ وَٱشۡهَدُوٓاْ أَنِّي بَرِيٓءٞ مِّمَّا تُشۡرِكُونَ ۝ مِن دُونِهِۦۖ فَكِيدُونِي جَمِيعٗا ثُمَّ لَا تُنظِرُونِ ۝ إِنِّي تَوَكَّلۡتُ عَلَى ٱللَّهِ رَبِّي وَرَبِّكُمۚ ...﴾

﴿... نَجَّيْنَا هُودًا وَٱلَّذِينَ ءَامَنُوا۟ مَعَهُۥ﴾

"Bear witness that I am absolved of the false gods that you partner with Allah. So plot against me collectively [if you will] and do not leave me. Indeed, I have put my trust in Allah, [Who is] my Lord and yours..."

"*...(And) We (Allah) saved Hūd and those who had embraced the faith with him...*"

(Qur'ān 11:54–58)

هِجَاءُ المشركين رسولَ الله ﷺ وستر الملائكة إيّاه

THE IDOLATORS' INSULTS TOWARDS THE MESSENGER OF ALLAH ﷺ AND THE ANGELS CONCEALING HIM

ḤADĪTH 36

عَنِ ابْنِ عَبَّاسٍ رضي الله عنهما، قَالَ: لَمَّا نَزَلَتْ: ﴿تَبَّتْ يَدَا أَبِي لَهَبٍ﴾ جَاءَتِ امْرَأَةُ أَبِي لَهَبٍ إِلَى النَّبِيِّ ﷺ، وَمَعَهُ أَبُو بَكْرٍ، فَلَمَّا رَآهَا أَبُو بَكْرٍ، قَالَ: يَا رَسُولَ اللهِ، إِنَّهَا امْرَأَةٌ بَذِيئَةٌ، وَأَخَافُ أَنْ تُؤْذِيَكَ، فَلَوْ قُمْتَ! قَالَ: إِنَّهَا لَنْ تَرَانِي، فَجَاءَتْ، فَقَالَتْ: يَا أَبَا بَكْرٍ، إِنَّ صَاحِبَكَ هَجَانِي، قَالَ: لَا، وَمَا يَقُولُ الشِّعْرَ، قَالَتْ: أَنْتَ عِنْدِي مُصَدَّقٌ، وَانْصَرَفَتْ، فَقُلْتُ: يَا رَسُولَ اللهِ، لَمْ تَرَكَ؟ قَالَ: لَا، لَمْ يَزَلْ مَلَكٌ يَسْتُرُنِي عَنْهَا بِجَنَاحِهِ.

(رواه ابن حبان في صحيحه)

Ibn ʿAbbās ﵁ narrates:

> When [the Sūrah], "May Abū Lahab perish…"[41] was revealed, the wife of Abū Lahab came to the Prophet ﷺ while Abū Bakr ﵁ was with him. When Abū Bakr saw her, he said, "O Messenger of Allah, she is a foul-mouthed woman and I fear that she will harm you. Won't you leave [from here]?" [The Messenger of Allah ﷺ] replied, "She will never see me." So, when she arrived, she said, "O Abū Bakr! Your companion has ridiculed me [through his poetry]!" He replied, "No, [he has not, because] he does not recite poetry."[42] She said, "I consider you to be a truthful person," and she departed. I (Ibn ʿAbbās ﵁) asked, "O Messenger of Allah, she couldn't see you?" He replied, "No, an angel continued to conceal me from her with its wing."
>
> (Ibn Ḥibbān)

Commentary

These days we may find ourselves facing all sorts of ridicule and insult. Sometimes, we must bear hateful words by random people in the community or through the Islamophobic rhetoric spewed by the media. As Muslims we have been

---

41 Qurʾān 111

42 What she is referring to is *hijāʾ*, a specific form of ridicule that is done through poetry.

given honor and dignity and as human beings we naturally feel pain. So, it is only normal to feel disheartened in these situations. We must therefore remind ourselves that even the Prophet ﷺ himself was not spared from this kind of insult and mockery. If he experienced it, it is inevitable that his true followers will experience the same.

﴿وَلَتَسْمَعُنَّ مِنَ ٱلَّذِينَ أُوتُوا۟ ٱلْكِتَٰبَ مِن قَبْلِكُمْ
وَمِنَ ٱلَّذِينَ أَشْرَكُوٓا۟ أَذًى كَثِيرًا ۚ﴾

"You will certainly hear from the people who received the revelation before you and from the idolaters many hurtful things."

(Qur'ān 3:186)

Our approach should not be to change our identity as Muslims, compromise our belief, or back out of our faith; rather, we should realize that insults and hurtful words will come and our ideal response is what Allah ﷻ Himself has advised us:

﴿وَٱصْبِرْ عَلَىٰ مَا يَقُولُونَ وَٱهْجُرْهُمْ هَجْرًا جَمِيلًا﴾

"And be patient over what they say and avoid them graciously."

(Qur'ān 73:10)

Along with the reassurance found in the verses:

﴿إِنَّ ٱلَّذِينَ أَجْرَمُوا۟ كَانُوا۟ مِنَ ٱلَّذِينَ ءَامَنُوا۟ يَضْحَكُونَ ۞ وَإِذَا مَرُّوا۟ بِهِمْ
يَتَغَامَزُونَ ۞ وَإِذَا ٱنقَلَبُوٓا۟ إِلَىٰٓ أَهْلِهِمُ ٱنقَلَبُوا۟ فَكِهِينَ ۞ وَإِذَا رَأَوْهُمْ قَالُوٓا۟
إِنَّ هَٰٓؤُلَآءِ لَضَآلُّونَ ۞ وَمَآ أُرْسِلُوا۟ عَلَيْهِمْ حَٰفِظِينَ ۞ فَٱلْيَوْمَ ٱلَّذِينَ
ءَامَنُوا۟ مِنَ ٱلْكُفَّارِ يَضْحَكُونَ ۞ عَلَى ٱلْأَرَآئِكِ يَنظُرُونَ ۞ هَلْ ثُوِّبَ
ٱلْكُفَّارُ مَا كَانُوا۟ يَفْعَلُونَ﴾

"Those in sin used to laugh at those who believed, and whenever they passed by them, they would wink at each other (in mockery). And when they returned to their own people, they would return jesting. And whenever they saw them, they would say, 'Behold! These are the people truly astray!' But they had not been sent as keepers over them! But on this Day (the Day of Judgment) the Believers will laugh at the Disbelievers: On Thrones (of Dignity) they will command a sight (of all things). Will not the disbelievers be paid back for what they did?"

(Qur'an 83:29–36)

أشدّ يومٍ مرَّ على رسول الله ﷺ

The Most Difficult Day for the Messenger of Allah ﷺ

Ḥadīth 37

عَنْ عَائِشَةَ رضي الله عنها أَنَّهَا قَالَتْ لِلنَّبِيِّ ﷺ: هَلْ أَتَى عَلَيْكَ يَوْمٌ كَانَ أَشَدَّ مِنْ يَوْمِ أُحُدٍ، قَالَ: لَقَدْ لَقِيتُ مِنْ قَوْمِكِ مَا لَقِيتُ، وَكَانَ أَشَدَّ مَا لَقِيتُ مِنْهُمْ يَوْمَ العَقَبَةِ، إِذْ عَرَضْتُ نَفْسِي عَلَى ابْنِ عَبْدِ يَالِيلَ بْنِ عَبْدِ كُلاَلٍ، فَلَمْ يُجِبْنِي إِلَى مَا أَرَدْتُ، فَانْطَلَقْتُ وَأَنَا مَهْمُومٌ عَلَى وَجْهِي، فَلَمْ أَسْتَفِقْ إِلاَّ وَأَنَا بِقَرْنِ الثَّعَالِبِ فَرَفَعْتُ رَأْسِي، فَإِذَا أَنَا بِسَحَابَةٍ قَدْ أَظَلَّتْنِي، فَنَظَرْتُ فَإِذَا فِيهَا جِبْرِيلُ، فَنَادَانِي فَقَالَ: إِنَّ اللهَ قَدْ سَمِعَ قَوْلَ قَوْمِكَ لَكَ، وَمَا رَدُّوا عَلَيْكَ، وَقَدْ بَعَثَ إِلَيْكَ مَلَكَ الجِبَالِ لِتَأْمُرَهُ بِمَا شِئْتَ فِيهِمْ، فَنَادَانِي مَلَكُ الجِبَالِ فَسَلَّمَ عَلَيَّ، ثُمَّ قَالَ: يَا مُحَمَّدُ، فَقَالَ، ذَلِكَ فِيمَا شِئْتَ، إِنْ شِئْتَ أَنْ أُطْبِقَ عَلَيْهِمُ الأَخْشَبَيْنِ؟ **فَقَالَ النَّبِيُّ ﷺ:** بَلْ أَرْجُو أَنْ يُخْرِجَ اللهُ مِنْ أَصْلاَبِهِمْ مَنْ يَعْبُدُ اللهَ وَحْدَهُ، لاَ يُشْرِكُ بِهِ شَيْئًا.

(متفق عليه)

ʿĀʾisha narrates that she asked the Prophet ﷺ:

"Was there any day more difficult for you than the day of Uḥud?" He said, "I endured from your people what I endured, but the most difficult day I experienced was the Day of ʿAqaba: when I had presented myself to Ibn ʿAbd Yalīl ibn ʿAbd Kulāl, but he did not respond to what I proposed.[43] So I left, overcome with grief, and I did not come out of that state of distress until I reached Qarn al-Thaʿālib.[44] When I looked up, I noticed a cloud was shading me. I looked towards it and suddenly realized that Jibrīl was in the cloud. He called out to me and said, 'Verily, Allah heard what your people said to you and how they rebuked you! So, Allah has sent the angel of the mountain to you that you may command him to do whatever you want to them.' The angel of the mountain called out to me, greeted me and said, 'O Muḥammad! [I will do] whatever you want. If you want, I can collapse upon them the two mountains [surrounding them].'" So, the Prophet ﷺ said, "No, rather I hope that Allah will bring forth from their offspring those who will worship Allah alone, without ascribing any partners to Him."

(Bukhārī and Muslim)

---

43 Meaning the call and invitation to Islam.

44 The *mīqāt* of the people coming to Makkah from Najd, also known as Qarn al-Manāzil (*Mirqāt al-Mafātīḥ Sharḥ Mishkāt al-Maṣābīḥ*). The *mīqāt* is a sacred boundary wherein a person must ready himself before entering the santified precinct of Makkah.

Commentary

The day that the Messenger of Allah ﷺ is making reference to is the day he was driven out of Ṭā'if. This was a harrowing day, wherein the Prophet was abused like on no other day.

After the passing of Abū Ṭālib, the Quraysh intensified their efforts against the Messenger of Allah ﷺ. The Prophet sought a refuge for the Muslims, where they would be left to practice their *dīn* freely. This lead him to Ṭā'if, a city belonging to the tribe of Thaqīf. He presented Islam to the leaders of the tribe and sought assistance from them. However, they scoffed at his invitation to Islam and refused his requests.

Then, the chiefs riled up the slaves and the most insolent people of their tribe to ridicule and jeer at the Messenger of Allah ﷺ. As the Messenger fled from the city, a crowd formed surrounding him on both sides. They mercilessly stoned him from behind, until his legs bled so profusely that his sandals were stained with blood. Finally, he escaped to a garden outside of the city and the crowd relented.[45]

After encountering all of this, the Messenger of Allah ﷺ supplicated to Allah ﷻ:

---

45 Taken from *Tārīkh al-Islām, Mirqāt al-Mafātīḥ Sharḥ Mishkāt al-Maṣābīḥ, al-Sīrah al-Ḥalabiyyah,* and *al-Rawḍ al-Unf.*

اَللّٰهُمَّ إِنِّيْ أَشْكُوْ إِلَيْكَ ضَعْفَ قُوَّتِيْ وَهَوَانِيْ عَلَى النَّاسِ. يَا أَرْحَمَ الرَّاحِمِيْنَ إِلَى مَنْ تَكِلُنِيْ، إِلَى عَدُوٍّ يَتَجَهَّمُنِيْ أَمْ إِلَى قَرِيْبٍ مَلَّكْتَهُ أَمْرِيْ؟ إِنْ لَمْ تَكُنْ غَضْبَانَ عَلَيَّ فَلَا أُبَالِيْ، غَيْرَ أَنَّ عَافِيَتَكَ أَوْسَعُ لِيْ. أَعُوْذُ بِوَجْهِكَ الَّذِيْ أَشْرَقَتْ لَهُ الظُّلُمَاتُ وَصَلُحَ عَلَيْهِ أَمْرُ الدُّنْيَا وَالْآخِرَةِ أَنْ يَنْزِلَ بِيْ غَضَبُكَ أَوْ يَحِلَّ بِيْ سَخَطُكَ. لَكَ الْعُتْبَى حَتَّى تَرْضَى، وَلَا قُوَّةَ إِلَّا بِاللّٰهِ.

"O Allah! To You do I complain about my lack of strength and my insignificance in the eyes of the people. O Most Merciful of those who show mercy! To whom will You entrust me? To an enemy who will deal with me with harshness? Or to a friend to whom You have assigned my affair? As long as You are not angry with me, then I have no concern; however, if You provide me with wellbeing then it is easier upon me. I seek refuge in [the Radiance of] Your Countenance—by which all darkness is removed, and the matters of this life and the next are made right—that neither Your anger nor Your wrath descend upon me. To You alone belongs all submission and recourse, so that You may be pleased. There is no might except with Allah."[46]

---

46 Narrated by Ṭabarānī and authenticated by Haythamī.

After the humiliation and suffering he faced at hands of the people of Ṭā'if, look at the humble words the Messenger ﷺ offers in supplication to Allah. He does not complain even once about the insult and abuse that he faced; his only concern being the pleasure of Allah. Who other than the Most Beloved of Allah could teach this degree of modesty before the Creator? After understanding the background behind this ḥadīth, we see that it clearly demonstrates how the Messenger of Allah ﷺ was the epitome of Allah's mercy upon His creation.

As Allah ﷻ has said:

﴿وَمَآ أَرۡسَلۡنَٰكَ إِلَّا رَحۡمَةٗ لِّلۡعَٰلَمِينَ﴾

"And we have not sent you but as a mercy for the worlds."

(Qur'an 21:107)

And as the Prophet ﷺ has mentioned, "I am but a mercy bestowed."[47]

If someone were to ask, "How was the Messenger of Allah ﷺ a mercy for the worlds? How was he a mercy bestowed upon

47 Al-Dārimī

mankind?" This incident alone serves as a sufficient answer, as it vividly encapsulates the words above with a physical example from the life of the Prophet ﷺ. Far from seeking revenge for the ordeal that he faced, his attitude towards his tormentors remained one of hope and wellwishing for their future generations.

What we should take from this ḥadīth is that when people are attacking us and ridiculing us, we should not look at them in their current state. We should have the foresight to see what they can become and what potential Allah may have instilled within them. No matter how externally ignorant, lost, or hateful a person may seem, there is always hope for that person's guidance. People are treasuries of beautiful qualities, like mines of gold and silver. They are treasure-troves of virtue and character and only a patient miner who painstakingly digs deep past all the dirt and rock, with forbearance, will get to the precious gems.

Before embracing Islam, ʿUmar opposed the Messenger of Allah ﷺ, but the Messenger ﷺ continued to make duʿāʾ for him because he saw his tremendous potential. The same was true with Khālid ibn Walīd. These are just two examples of people—from amongst hundreds—who started out as staunch enemies, but through the foresight of the Prophet ﷺ—coupled with his forbearance, mercy, and compassion

—one became "al-Fārūq"[48] and the other became "Sayfullah,"[49] may Allah be pleased with them both.

Let us not be people who only see the external, materialistic perspective of things, who see nothing but what is immediately before their eyes. The result of the Prophet's ﷺ mercy and forbearance was that the same people who had turned him out and expelled him from his city, not only accepted Islam, but became a means of guidance for many people after them.

48 Meaning, "the Criterion between Truth and Falsehood." The title given to ʿUmar ﵁ by the Messenger of Allah ﷺ.

49 Meaning, "the Sword of Allah." The title given to Khālid ﵁ by the Messenger of Allah ﷺ.

تحمّله ﷺ اِغتيالات اليهود و شرورهم

His ﷺ Enduring the Assassination Attempts of Some of the Jews and Their Evils

Ḥadīth 38

عَنْ أَبِي هُرَيْرَةَ رضي الله عنه قَالَ: كَانَ رَسُولُ اللهِ ﷺ يَأْكُلُ الْهَدِيَّةَ، وَلَا يَأْكُلُ الصَّدَقَةَ.

وَ فِي مَوْضِعٍ آخَرَ زاد الراوي مرسلا: فَأَهْدَتْ لَهُ يَهُودِيَّةٌ بِخَيْبَرَ شَاةً مَصْلِيَّةً سَمَّتْهَا، فَأَكَلَ رَسُولُ اللهِ ﷺ مِنْهَا وَأَكَلَ الْقَوْمُ، فَقَالَ: ارْفَعُوا أَيْدِيَكُمْ فَإِنَّهَا أَخْبَرَتْنِي أَنَّهَا مَسْمُومَةٌ، فَمَاتَ بِشْرُ بْنُ الْبَرَاءِ بْنِ مَعْرُورٍ الْأَنْصَارِيُّ، فَأَرْسَلَ إِلَى الْيَهُودِيَّةِ: مَا حَمَلَكِ عَلَى الَّذِي صَنَعْتِ؟ قَالَتْ: إِنْ كُنْتَ نَبِيًّا لَمْ يَضُرَّكَ الَّذِي صَنَعْتُ، وَإِنْ كُنْتَ مَلِكًا أَرَحْتُ النَّاسَ مِنْكَ، فَأَمَرَ بِهَا رَسُولُ اللهِ ﷺ فَقُتِلَتْ، ثُمَّ قَالَ فِي وَجَعِهِ الَّذِي مَاتَ فِيهِ: مَا زِلْتُ أَجِدُ مِنَ الْأَكْلَةِ الَّتِي أَكَلْتُ بِخَيْبَرَ، فَهَذَا أَوَانُ قَطَعَتْ أَبْهَرِي.

(رواه أبي داود)

Abū Hurayra ؓ narrates:

> The Messenger of Allah ﷺ would accept gifts but he would not accept any charity [for himself].

The narrator adds:

> Once a Jewish woman from Khaybar gifted him a roasted sheep that she had poisoned. The Messenger of Allah ﷺ [unknowingly] ate from it along with some of the people. Suddenly he said, "Lift your hands [from the food], because it has informed me that it is poisoned!"[50] As a result [of the poisoning], Bishr ibn al-Barāʾ ibn Maʿrūr al-Anṣārī died. So, the Messenger of Allah ﷺ inquired from the Jewish woman, "What prompted you to do this?" She replied, "If you were truly a prophet, it would not harm you. And if you were just some king, then I would have relieved the people of you." The Messenger of Allah ﷺ ordered that she be killed [for her crime]. Years later, he said during his [final] illness from which he passed away, "I still feel pain from that [poisoned] morsel that I ate in Khaybar. And now its [poison] has severed my life-line!"[51]

(Abū Dāwūd)

---

[50] This was a miracle of the Prophet ﷺ.

[51] An expression meaning "it has killed me."

Commentary

The Prophet ﷺ ordered that the woman should be killed due to her murdering the Ṣaḥābī and attempting to murder everyone else. This was based on the law of *qiṣāṣ* (punishment for murder).[52]

HADĪTH 39

عَنْ عَائِشَةَ رضي الله عنها قَالَتْ: سَحَرَ رَسُولَ اللهِ ﷺ رَجُلٌ مِنْ بَنِي زُرَيْقٍ، يُقَالُ لَهُ لَبِيدُ بْنُ الأَعْصَمِ، حَتَّى كَانَ رَسُولُ اللهِ ﷺ يُخَيَّلُ إِلَيْهِ أَنَّهُ كَانَ يَفْعَلُ الشَّيْءَ وَمَا فَعَلَهُ، حَتَّى إِذَا كَانَ ذَاتَ يَوْمٍ أَوْ ذَاتَ لَيْلَةٍ وَهُوَ عِنْدِي، لَكِنَّهُ دَعَا وَدَعَا، ثُمَّ قَالَ: يَا عَائِشَةُ، أَشَعَرْتِ أَنَّ اللهَ أَفْتَانِي فِيمَا اسْتَفْتَيْتُهُ فِيهِ، أَتَانِي رَجُلَانِ، فَقَعَدَ أَحَدُهُمَا عِنْدَ رَأْسِي، وَالآخَرُ عِنْدَ رِجْلَيَّ، فَقَالَ أَحَدُهُمَا لِصَاحِبِهِ: مَا وَجَعُ الرَّجُلِ؟ فَقَالَ: مَطْبُوبٌ، قَالَ: مَنْ طَبَّهُ؟ قَالَ: لَبِيدُ بْنُ الأَعْصَمِ،

52 This is the punishment for murder that is found in both Islamic and Jewish laws.

قَالَ: فِي أَيِّ شَيْءٍ؟ قَالَ: فِي مُشْطٍ وَمُشَاطَةٍ، وَجُفِّ طَلْعِ نَخْلَةٍ ذَكَرٍ، قَالَ: وَأَيْنَ هُوَ؟ قَالَ: فِي بِئْرِ ذَرْوَانَ، فَأَتَاهَا رَسُولُ اللهِ ﷺ فِي نَاسٍ مِنْ أَصْحَابِهِ، فَجَاءَ فَقَالَ: يَا عَائِشَةُ، كَأَنَّ مَاءَهَا نُقَاعَةُ الحِنَّاءِ، أَوْ كَأَنَّ رُءُوسَ نَخْلِهَا رُءُوسُ الشَّيَاطِينِ، قُلْتُ: يَا رَسُولَ اللهِ: أَفَلاَ اسْتَخْرَجْتَهُ؟ قَالَ: قَدْ عَافَانِي اللهُ، فَكَرِهْتُ أَنْ أُثَوِّرَ عَلَى النَّاسِ فِيهِ شَرًّا. فَأَمَرَ بِهَا فَدُفِنَتْ.

(رواه البخاري)

ʿĀʾISHA ﷺ NARRATES:

A man from Banī Zurayq known as Labīd ibn al-Aʿṣam performed sorcery[53] upon the Messenger of Allah ﷺ to such an extent that the Prophet would think he had done things that in reality he had not done. This continued for some time until once—when he was with me—he continued to supplicate and supplicate until he called out, "O ʿĀʾisha! Do you know how Allah has answered me in regards to what I have been inquiring about? Two men came to me. One of them

53 Black magic or *siḥr*.

sat near my head and the other near my feet. One of them asked the other, 'What ails this man?' The other said, 'He is under the effects of sorcery.' The first one asked, 'Who has performed this upon him?' To which the other replied, 'Labīd ibn al-Aʿṣam.' The first further inquired, 'What was used to do this sorcery?' The other replied, 'A comb, the hair stuck to it, and the hollowed-out sheath of a date palm.' The first asked, 'And where is it located?' The other replied, 'In the well of Dharwān.'" The Messenger of Allah ﷺ and a group of his companions went to it, and when the Messenger returned he said, "O ʿĀ'isha! The water of the well looks like the leftover water from the dye of henna."[54] Or he said, "The tops of the date palms [surrounding it] are [spiky] like the heads of the devils."

I (ʿĀ'isha) asked, "O Messenger of Allah, why did you not show it to the people?" He replied, "Allah has granted me wellbeing, and I do not want evil to spread amongst the people because of it." Then, he commanded that the well be filled with dirt.

(Bukhārī)

[54] A brownish-red dye made from the leaves of a tree by the same name.

Commentary

This ḥadīth demonstrates that the evil effect of black magic is real and can hurt a person. Allah ﷻ speaks of this in the Qurʾān:

﴿فَيَتَعَلَّمُونَ مِنْهُمَا مَا يُفَرِّقُونَ بِهِۦ بَيْنَ ٱلْمَرْءِ وَزَوْجِهِۦ ۚ
وَمَا هُم بِضَآرِّينَ بِهِۦ مِنْ أَحَدٍ إِلَّا بِإِذْنِ ٱللَّهِ ۚ﴾

"So they learn that which causes separation between husband and wife, however, they could not harm anyone except by Allah's permission."

(Qurʾān 2:102)

We have also previously mentioned that anything that can hurt a normal person can affect the Messenger of Allah ﷺ as well. One of the reasons why the Prophet ﷺ experienced such a wide array of tribulations and difficulties was likely because Allah had chosen him as an *uswa* (exemplar) for all of mankind. His example was not restricted to his time, ethnicity, gender, or background.

Some people become confused as to how the Messenger ﷺ could be affected by black-magic, whereas if he was sent by Allah, how could he be affected by such things?

Answering this doubt, Imām Ibn al-Qayyim writes in *Zād al-Maʿād*, "Some people reject the fact that the Messenger of Allah can be affected by black-magic and have said, 'it is not permissible for this to happen to the Prophet,' [because] they consider it to be a deficiency and weakness. But they have misunderstood this matter, because [in reality] this issue is similar to all the other ailments that affected him... Its effect was similar to the poison which was given to him. There is no difference between the two."

Qāḍī ʿIyāḍ mentions in his *al-Shifā*, "The effects of black-magic manifest like an ailment and it is also categorized as such. This is something that *can* happen to the Prophet and does not affect his prophethood or the divine revelation." As the ultimate role-model for all humankind, it was only inevitable that the Prophet Muḥammad ﷺ endure all the physical, emotional, and spiritual hardships that people experience in life. May Allah shower upon him perpetual blessings and mercy for eternity.

تحمّله ﷺ أذيّة المنافقين

The Prophet ﷺ Tolerating the harm Inflicted upon Him by the Hypocrites

Ḥadīth 40

قَالَتْ أُمُّ الْمُؤْمِنِينَ عَائِشَةُ رضي الله عنها حَاكِيَةً عَنْ وَاقِعَةِ الْإِفْكِ: فَقَامَ رَسُولُ اللهِ ﷺ مِنْ يَوْمِهِ فَاسْتَعْذَرَ مِنْ عَبْدِ اللهِ بْنِ أُبَيٍّ، وَهُوَ عَلَى الْمِنْبَرِ، فَقَالَ: يَا مَعْشَرَ الْمُسْلِمِينَ، مَنْ يَعْذِرُنِي مِنْ رَجُلٍ قَدْ بَلَغَنِي عَنْهُ أَذَاهُ فِي أَهْلِي، وَاللهِ مَا عَلِمْتُ عَلَى أَهْلِي إِلَّا خَيْرًا، وَلَقَدْ ذَكَرُوا رَجُلًا مَا عَلِمْتُ عَلَيْهِ إِلَّا خَيْرًا، وَمَا يَدْخُلُ عَلَى أَهْلِي إِلَّا مَعِي...

(رواه البخاري)

ʿĀʾisha رضي الله عنها narrates regarding the incident of *Ifk*:

The Messenger of Allah ﷺ stood upon the *mimbar* one day and sought relief from ʿAbdullah ibn Ubayy, saying, "O Muslims! Who will grant me relief from such a person who has harmed me by hurting my family. By Allah, I know nothing of my family except good. And they have also accused a man (Safwān ibn Muʿaṭṭal) of whom I know nothing except good and who does not enter my house except in my company..."

(Bukhārī)

COMMENTARY

In the incident of *ifk* (defamation), the *munāfiqīn* (hypocrites) were looking to hurt the Prophet ﷺ and his family with a personal attack. They waited for the right moment and spun the situation into a false, scandalous story thereby intending to defame the honor of the Prophet ﷺ and his family. The Prophet ﷺ and the Ṣaḥābah were returning to Madīnah in a caravan. They made a routine stop, during which ʿĀʾisha ﵢ left her covered carriage atop her camel to answer the call of nature. The carriages were covered to prevent anyone from seeing the woman inside, hence no one could tell that she had left. Since it was assumed she was still inside, when the caravan resumed moving forward, she was accidentally left behind.

It was protocol for caravans to have a person follow from a distance; if someone or something was left behind, they would then be able to assist. Ṣafwān ibn al-Muʿaṭṭal ﵢ was that man for this caravan, and he found that ʿĀʾisha ﵢ had been accidentally left behind. He allowed her to sit atop the camel while he led by walking a significant distance ahead of her. He never turned back to look at the Mother of the Believers.[55] In this way he led her all the way home.

This was the situation that the hypocrites—led by ʿAbdullah ibn Ubayy ibn Salūl—took advantage of, by fabricating lies and accusing the noble family of the Prophet ﷺ of adultery. When they entered back into the city, these hypocrites said, "Look at them, how they are coming together without anyone else with them! There must be something going on between them!" Unfortunately, some simple-minded believers fell into the trap of going along with this. A lot of gossip ensued in Madīnah due to this, but eventually Allah ﷻ Himself—through divine revelation—cleared the name of ʿĀʾisha Ṣiddīqa ﵂ and elevated her rank through this whole ordeal.[56] The true face of the hypocrites became exposed in the end, as Allah mentions:

﴿إِنَّ ٱلَّذِينَ جَآءُو بِٱلۡإِفۡكِ عُصۡبَةٞ مِّنكُمۡۚ لَا تَحۡسَبُوهُ شَرّٗا لَّكُمۖ بَلۡ هُوَ خَيۡرٞ لَّكُمۡۚ﴾

"Surely those who concocted and spread the slander (against ʿĀʾisha ﵂, the Messenger's ﷺ wife) are a band from amongst you. However, do not deem this incident evil for you; rather, it is good for you."

(Qurʾan 24:11)

55 A title of honor given to the wives of the Prophet ﷺ.

56 Qurʾān 24: 26

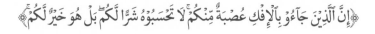

Allah ﷻ elucidates that in this incredibly difficult test there is actually hidden good. We can imagine the pain and emotional stress that such an accusation can bring upon a person. Think of how it hurt ʿĀʾisha Ṣiddīqa ؓ, who mentioned, "… the tears from my eyes would not stop flowing."[57] Imagine the emotional trauma it caused the Messenger of Allah ﷺ himself. Consider how much this hurt Abū Bakr ؓ and his noble and pure family. All of this may make a person think to themselves: what inherent good can there possibly be in this?!

We learn many lessons from this incident, but the most important lesson to be taken from traumatizing situations like this is that even though we may assume that these incidents hurt us, the reward and benefit that returns back to us is far greater. Shaykh Aḥmad ibn ʿAjība al-Maghribī mentions in his *tafsīr*, *Al-Baḥr al-Madīd*:

> The inherent good that was in this apparent incident of defamation the Prophet ﷺ and his family was that it resulted in:
>
> - Attaining great reward by patiently bearing this hardship.
> - Manifesting the honor that these people had in Allah's sight.

57 Bukhārī

- The revelation of verses of the Qur'ān—which will be recited until the Day of Judgment—to clear their name and elevate their status.
- Extolling those who continued to have a good opinion of them despite the accusations.
- An earnest desire to turn to Allah for succor.
- A state of longing for Allah's mercy.
- A hopelessness and detachment from the creation.

After learning about the public and private struggles faced by the Prophet ﷺ and his family, can there be any excuse for us to complain and become bitter about our own problems?

اختفاؤه ﷺ في الغار و توكّله على الله

The Messenger ﷺ Relying upon Allah, While Hiding in the Cave of Thawr

Ḥadīth 41

عَنْ أَبِي بَكْرٍ رضي الله عنه، قَالَ: كُنْتُ مَعَ النَّبِيِّ ﷺ فِي الغَارِ فَرَأَيْتُ آثَارَ الْمُشْرِكِينَ، قُلْتُ: يَا رَسُولَ اللهِ، لَوْ أَنَّ أَحَدَهُمْ رَفَعَ قَدَمَهُ رَآنَا، قَالَ: مَا ظَنُّكَ بِاثْنَيْنِ اللهُ ثَالِثُهُمَا.

(رواه البخاري)

Abū Bakr al-Ṣiddīq رضي الله عنه narrates:

I was with the Prophet ﷺ in the cave [of Thawr],[58] when I suddenly saw the feet of the idolators [who

58 After thirteen years of calling the people of Makkah to Islam in the face of staunch opposition and persecution, Allah commanded the believers to make *hijrah* (migrate) to Madīnah. On the night the Prophet ﷺ embarked on this journey, the Quraysh narrowly failed in an assassination attempt due to the divine protection of Allah. As a result, the Quraysh set a bounty upon the head of the Messenger of Allah ﷺ; making an already arduous journey all the more treacherous. To evade the pursuit of those chasing him, the Messenger of Allah ﷺ hid for three days in the Cave of Thawr—a tight cave to the south of Makkah. The only one to accompany him for the entire journey was Abū Bakr رضي الله عنه.

were pursuing us] and said, "O Messenger of Allah, if any of them were to lift up their foot, they would see us." The Prophet ﷺ said, "What do you think of those two, the third of whom is Allah?"

(Bukhārī)

Commentary

The help of Allah is near when one is all out of options. If the help came down before all of one's options were exhausted, then it would leave room for the notion that perhaps the victory was actually achieved through some worldly means (*asbāb*). Instead, Allah allows His slave to reach a point where he sees no way out, and then provides him with relief—so that the slave may realize with conviction that there is no helper or savior but Allah. This conviction serves to benefit none other than the slave himself, and this is the wisdom in the divine system of Allah.

The Messenger of Allah ﷺ taught the Ṣaḥābah to view every situation as one in which there is no other option besides turning to Allah. Thus, they would adopt whatever worldly means they could, without actually ever placing their hopes in those means. If anything, they were completely hopeless of the means, because their hope rested solely in Allah. The Messenger of Allah ﷺ taught the Ṣaḥābah to *begin* from that point of surrender—not just resort to it when there was no other option.

From this incident we also come to know of the status of Abū Bakr 🏵, his close relationship with the Prophet 🏵, and his deep love and concern for him. It should be known that during this event, Abū Bakr 🏵 was not scared for himself; rather, his concern and greatest struggle was for the well-being of the Messenger of Allah 🏵. He was granted the special status of "*Ṣiddīq*"[59] by Allah because he was the reflection and embodiment of the worry, concern, and effort of the Prophet 🏵. The ardent desire that Allah's *dīn* should prevail, the unending concern for the guidance and salvation of mankind, and the full understanding and realization of the objective of prophethood was the essence of the station of *Ṣiddīq*. Additionally, he knew that any injury or harm that would afflict the Messenger 🏵 would also, in effect, injure and harm the entire *dīn* of Allah. For this reason, he sacrificed his life, wealth, and everything beloved to him for the sake of Allah.

---

[59] Meaning, "the Eminently Veracious," the one who confirms the truth through word and deed. This was the title given to Abū Bakr 🏵.

تحمّله ﷺ أذي الجفاة و الجهّال و حِلْمُهُ عليهم

His ﷺ Enduring the Annoyances of the Ill-Mannered and the Ignorant, and His Forbearance with Them

Ḥadīth 42

عَنْ أَنَسِ بْنِ مَالِكٍ رضي الله عنه، قَالَ: كُنْتُ أَمْشِي مَعَ النَّبِيِّ ﷺ وَعَلَيْهِ بُرْدٌ نَجْرَانِيٌّ غَلِيظُ الحَاشِيَةِ، فَأَدْرَكَهُ أَعْرَابِيٌّ فَجَذَبَهُ جَذْبَةً شَدِيدَةً، حَتَّى نَظَرْتُ إِلَى صَفْحَةِ عَاتِقِ النَّبِيِّ ﷺ قَدْ أَثَّرَتْ بِهِ حَاشِيَةُ الرِّدَاءِ مِنْ شِدَّةِ جَذْبَتِهِ، ثُمَّ قَالَ: مُرْ لِي مِنْ مَالِ اللهِ الَّذِي عِنْدَكَ، فَالْتَفَتَ إِلَيْهِ فَضَحِكَ، ثُمَّ أَمَرَ لَهُ بِعَطَاءٍ.

(رواه مسلم)

Anas ibn Mālik رضي الله عنه narrates:

I was walking with the Prophet ﷺ while he was wearing a rough Najrānī[60] shawl with a very thick border. A bedouin caught up to him and yanked it so hard that

60 Made in Najrān, a region close to modern day Yemen.

I saw the shawl's border leave a mark on the neck of the Prophet ﷺ, due to how severely the bedouin had pulled the shawl. Then [the bedouin] said, "Give me [something] from the wealth of Allah which is in your possession." So [the Prophet ﷺ] turned towards him, laughed, and then ordered that the bedouin be given something.

(Muslim)

ḤADĪTH 43

عَنْ أَبِي هُرَيْرَةَ رضي الله عنه، قَالَ: دَخَلَ أَعْرَابِيٌّ الْمَسْجِدَ وَالنَّبِيُّ ﷺ جَالِسٌ، فَصَلَّى، فَلَمَّا فَرَغَ، قَالَ: اللَّهُمَّ ارْحَمْنِي وَمُحَمَّدًا وَلاَ تَرْحَمْ مَعَنَا أَحَدًا، فَالتَفَتَ إِلَيْهِ النَّبِيُّ ﷺ، فَقَالَ: لَقَدْ تَحَجَّرْتَ وَاسِعًا، فَلَمْ يَلْبَثْ أَنْ بَالَ فِي الْمَسْجِدِ، فَأَسْرَعَ إِلَيْهِ النَّاسُ، فَقَالَ النَّبِيُّ ﷺ: أَهْرِيقُوا عَلَيْهِ سَجْلاً مِنْ مَاءٍ، - أَوْ قال- دَلْوًا مِنْ مَاءٍ، ثُمَّ قَالَ: إِنَّمَا بُعِثْتُمْ مُيَسِّرِينَ وَلَمْ تُبْعَثُوا مُعَسِّرِينَ.

(رواه الترمذي)

Abū Hurayra ؓ narrates:

> A Bedouin entered the masjid while the Prophet ﷺ was sitting down. [The Bedouin] offered his prayer and, upon finishing, supplicated, "O Allah, have mercy upon me and Muḥammad and do not have mercy upon anyone else." The Prophet ﷺ turned towards him and said, "You have restricted something that is very vast." Not long after that, the Bedouin stood up and began urinating in the masjid. The people rushed towards him [to restrain him]. But the Prophet ﷺ [simply] said, "Pour a bucket of water over it." Thereafter he ﷺ said, "You have been sent to make things easy, you have not been sent to make things difficult."

(Tirmidhī)

Commentary

Regarding these ḥadīths, one of the characteristics of the Messenger of Allah ﷺ that becomes manifest is whenever someone asked him for something, he would give it if he had it. His generosity did not diminish, even if people behaved poorly with him. His ﷺ character was a shining star whether in ease or in difficulty, whether people were nice to him or rude.

We also learn how he would not allow the ignorance of others to bring him down to their level. He treated everyone according to his magnanimity and character, not according to their ignorance and lack of character. When someone attacks us with ill will or evil, we often instinctively respond in much the same way. However, the sublime character of the Prophet ﷺ teaches us the opposite of this, as Allah mentions in the Qur'ān,

﴿وَلَا تَسْتَوِي ٱلْحَسَنَةُ وَلَا ٱلسَّيِّئَةُ ٱدْفَعْ بِٱلَّتِي هِيَ أَحْسَنُ فَإِذَا ٱلَّذِي بَيْنَكَ وَبَيْنَهُۥ عَدَٰوَةٌ كَأَنَّهُۥ وَلِيٌّ حَمِيمٌ ۝ وَمَا يُلَقَّىٰهَآ إِلَّا ٱلَّذِينَ صَبَرُوا۟ وَمَا يُلَقَّىٰهَآ إِلَّا ذُو حَظٍّ عَظِيمٍ﴾

"Good and evil [conduct] are not equal. Repel [evil] with what is best. [If you do so,] behold, he whom between you and him was enmity, will be as though he were a sympathetic friend. And none are ever enabled to attain it (such great virtue) except those who are patient; and none are ever enabled to attain it except those who have good fortune."

(Qur'ān 41:34–35)

GRIEF & PERSONAL LOSS EXPERIENCED BY THE BELOVED PROPHET

صلى الله عليه وآله وسلم

استشهاده عمّه حمزة بن عبد المطلب و شدّة حُزنه ﷺ عليه

The Martyrdom of His ﷺ Uncle, Ḥamza ibn ʿAbd al-Muṭṭalib, and the Severity of the Prophet's Grief over Him.

Ḥadīth 44

عَنْ أَنَسٍ رضي الله عنه قَالَ: لَمَّا كَانَ يَوْمُ أُحُدٍ مَرَّ رَسُولُ اللهِ ﷺ بِحَمْزَةَ وَقَدْ جُدِعَ أَنْفُهُ وَمُثِّلَ بِهِ فَقَالَ: لَوْلَا أَنْ تَجِدَ صَفِيَّةُ فِي نَفْسِهَا تَرَكْتُهُ حَتَّى يَحْشُرَهُ اللهُ مِنْ بُطُونِ السِّبَاعِ وَالطَّيْرِ. فَكُفِّنَ فِي نَمِرَةٍ، إِذَا خُمِّرَ رَأْسُهُ بَدَتْ رِجْلَاهُ وَإِذَا خُمِّرَتْ رِجْلَاهُ بَدَا رَأْسُهُ، فَخَمَّرُوا رَأْسَهُ ...

(رواه أبو يعلى في مسنده وقال الهيثمي: رجاله رجال الصحيح)

Ḥadīth 45

وَفِي مَرَاسِيلِ أَبِي دَاود: صَلَّى النَّبِيُّ ﷺ عَلَى حَمْزَةَ يَوْمَ أُحُدٍ سَبْعِينَ صَلَاةً بَدْءًا بِحَمْزَةَ فَصَلَّى عَلَيْهِ، ثُمَّ جَعَلَ يَدْعُو بِالشُّهَدَاءِ فَيُصَلِّي عَلَيْهِمْ، وَحَمْزَةُ مَكَانَهُ.

ḤADĪTH 46

وَفِيْ مُسْنَدِ أَحْمَدَ عَنْ عَبْدِ اللهِ بْنِ عُمَرَ ﵄: أَنَّ رَسُولَ اللهِ ﷺ لَمَّا رَجَعَ مِنْ أُحُدٍ، فَجَعَلَتْ نِسَاءُ الْأَنْصَارِ يَبْكِينَ عَلَى مَنْ قُتِلَ مِنْ أَزْوَاجِهِنَّ، قَالَ: فَقَالَ رَسُولُ اللهِ ﷺ: وَلَكِنْ حَمْزَةُ لَا بَوَاكِيَ لَهُ. قَالَ: ثُمَّ نَامَ فَاسْتَنْبَهَ وَهُنَّ يَبْكِينَ قَالَ: فَهُنَّ الْيَوْمَ إِذًا يَبْكِينَ

يَنْدُبْنَ بِحَمْزَةَ.

ANAS ﵁ NARRATES:

On the day of Uḥud, the Prophet ﷺ passed by Ḥamza's body; his nose was cut off and his body was severely mutilated. [Seeing this,] the Messenger of Allah ﷺ said, "If Ṣafiyya[61] would not be saddened by it, I would have left his body [in this condition] so that he would be resurrected by Allah [on the Day of Judgment] from the stomachs of the wild animals and birds." Thereafter, Ḥamza was shrouded in a thick cotton sheet that [was so short,] if it was used to cover his head, his legs would be exposed; and if it was used to cover his feet, his head would be exposed. So, they [decided] to cover his head with it.

(Abu Yaʿlā)

---

61 Ṣafiyya ﵂ was the sister of Ḥamza ﵁ and the aunt of the Messenger of Allah ﷺ. Both embraced Islam, and were very dear to the Messenger of Allah.

In a mursal narration of Abū Dāwūd it is mentioned:

> On the day of Uḥud, the Messenger of Allah ﷺ prayed upon Ḥamza seventy times. He began by first praying over the body of Ḥamza alone, then he prayed for each of the martyrs while Ḥamza's body remained in its place.

In a narration of ʿAbdullah ibn ʿUmar narrated by Imām Aḥmad in the Musnad:

> When the Messenger of Allah ﷺ returned from Uḥud, the women of the Anṣār began crying over their husbands that were killed in battle. The Prophet ﷺ remarked, "As for Ḥamza, there is no one to mourn his death." ʿAbdullah continued, "Then the Prophet ﷺ took a nap and was awakened by the crying of the Anṣārī women. [Hearing this] the Prophet ﷺ said, "Now when they mourn, they remember and lament the loss of Ḥamza."

Commentary

Ḥamza ؓ grew up with the Messenger of Allah ﷺ and was like a brother to him. Despite Ḥamza ؓ being his uncle, they were very close in age and were foster brothers.[62] Ḥamza's ؓ embracing of Islam was a great bounty for the Muslims

62 *Riḍāʿī* brothers. They were both suckled by the same wet-nurse, which Islamically forms an additional bond of kinship.

and a catalyst for increasing the morale of the believers. His loss was very difficult on the Messenger of Allah ﷺ, as is apparent from this ḥadīth.

Even though Ḥamza ؓ made the ultimate sacrifice in the path of Allah, this does not take away from the grief the Messenger of Allah ﷺ is experiencing. His statement about the birds and animals was a desire to elevate and multiply the rewards and honor for the martyrdom of his beloved uncle. He desired that on the Day of Judgment, all of creation bear witness to the immense sacrifice that Ḥamza had made.

The Prophet's ﷺ grief and sadness for Ḥamza's ؓ state of loneliness and helplessness (i.e. not having anyone to mourn for him after his death) was an innate expression of the Prophet's compassion and mercy. This teaches the Ummah that sadness, grief and all the emotions that are felt when one loses a loved one are only natural. Even though we fully recognize the acceptance and great reward that is found in martyrdom, there is no harm in feeling pain when it happens to someone close to us. The Prophet ﷺ still expressed grief, cried, and was saddened over the loss of his loved ones, despite being the Prophet of Allah. We learn from the perfect example of the Prophet ﷺ that expressing emotions do not go against contentment with Allah's decree.

Later, we will see the boundaries of how to cope with this type of pain in the ḥadīth regarding the death of the Prophet's ﷺ son.

شدّة حُزنه ﷺ على فقدِ أُمّه و تذكّره ايّاها

The Severity of His ﷺ Grief over the Loss of His Mother and His Remembrance of Her

Ḥadīth 47

عَنِ ابْنِ مَسْعُودٍ رضي الله عنه، أَنَّ رَسُولَ اللهِ ﷺ خَرَجَ يَوْمًا، فَخَرَجْنَا مَعَهُ، حَتَّى انْتَهَيْنَا إِلَى الْمَقَابِرِ، فَأَمَرَنَا فَجَلَسْنَا، ثُمَّ تَخَطَّى الْقُبُورَ حَتَّى انْتَهَى إِلَى قَبْرٍ مِنْهَا فَجَلَسَ إِلَيْهِ، فَنَاجَاهُ طَوِيلًا، ثُمَّ رَجَعَ رَسُولُ اللهِ ﷺ بَاكِيًا، فَبَكَيْنَا لِبُكَاءِ رَسُولِ اللهِ ﷺ، ثُمَّ أَقْبَلَ عَلَيْنَا، فَتَلَقَّاهُ عُمَرُ رِضْوَانُ اللهِ عَلَيْهِ وَقَالَ: مَا الَّذِي أَبْكَاكَ يَا رَسُولَ اللهِ، فَقَدْ أَبْكَيْتَنَا وَأَفْزَعْتَنَا؟ فَأَخَذَ بِيَدِ عُمَرَ، ثُمَّ أَقْبَلَ عَلَيْنَا، فَقَالَ: أَفْزَعَكُمْ بُكَائِي؟ قُلْنَا: نَعَمْ, فَقَالَ: إِنَّ الْقَبْرَ الَّذِي رَأَيْتُمُونِي أُنَاجِي قَبْرُ آمِنَةَ بِنْتِ وَهْبٍ، وَإِنِّي سَأَلْتُ رَبِّي الِاسْتِغْفَارَ

لَهَا، فَلَمْ يَأْذَنْ لِي، فَنَزَلَ عَلَيَّ: ﴿مَا كَانَ لِلنَّبِيِّ وَالَّذِينَ آمَنُوا أَنْ يَسْتَغْفِرُوا

لِلْمُشْرِكِينَ﴾ فَأَخَذَنِي مَا يَأْخُذُ الْوَلَدُ لِلْوَالِدِ مِنَ الرِّقَةِ، فَذَلِكَ الَّذِي

أَبْكَانِي، أَلَا وَإِنِّي كُنْتُ نَهَيْتُكُمْ عَنْ زِيَارَةِ الْقُبُورِ، فَزُورُوهَا، فَإِنَّهَا

تُزَهِّدُ فِي الدُّنْيَا وَتُرَغِّبُ فِي الْآخِرَةِ.

(رواه ابن حبان في صحيحه)

ʿABDULLAH IBN MASʿŪD 🖌 NARRATES:

One day we set out with the Messenger of Allah 🖌 until we reached a graveyard. He commanded us to sit, so we sat. He 🖌 began walking through the graveyard until he reached one of the graves. He sat facing it and began to whisper to it for a long time. After some time, the Messenger of Allah 🖌 returned to us weeping, so we also began to weep due to the weeping of the Messenger of Allah 🖌. He then turned towards us, and ʿUmar 🖌 greeted him and asked, "What has saddened you, O Messenger of Allah? Seeing your condition has made us weep and worried us." He then took hold of ʿUmar's hand and addressed us asking, "Has my crying worried you?" We replied, "Yes."

So, he explained, "The grave you witnessed me entreating upon was the grave of Āmina bint Wahb.[63] I asked my Lord for permission to seek forgiveness on her behalf, but I was not permitted to do so and the verse was revealed to me:

'It does not befit the Messenger, or those who believe, to seek forgiveness for the idolaters'[64]

Then the feelings that a child has for his mother overtook me and that is what caused me to weep."

"Take notice, I used to prevent you from the visiting the graves. However, now you should visit them, because it disinclines you from the world and creates a desire for the Hereafter."

(Ibn Ḥibbān)

Commentary

This ḥadīth raises the matter concerning the condition of the Prophet's ﷺ parents in the afterlife. What is specifically mentioned here is that *at this particular time* the Prophet ﷺ

63 The mother of the Messenger of Allah ﷺ.

64 Qur'ān 9: 113

was not allowed to make *istighfār*[65] for his mother. This does not necessarily provide any definitive proof regarding the final state of the Messenger's ﷺ mother. Ultimately, Allah alone is the judge. If we observe silence on this matter, we will not be held accountable either way because this is neither from the absolute essentials of Islamic creed that we are required to know as Muslims, nor is it from those matters that we will be asked about in the Hereafter. Scholars have differed about this issue and a ḥadīth has been narrated regarding it,[66] stating in effect that Allah restored the life of the Prophet's ﷺ parents after which they brought faith in him. However, many of the scholars of ḥadīth have categorized this narration as being fabricated.[67]

Others argue that the Prophet's ﷺ parents died in the period of *fatrah* (the period in which there was no revelation or prophet sent). Hence, they are not held accountable for "disbelief" and, therefore, are from the people of salvation. Still others say that all the Prophet's ﷺ forefathers were believers and never worshipped idols, hence, this also proves the salvation of his parents.

---

65 Seeking forgiveness from Allah.

66 One of those who narrate this ḥadīth is Imām Suyūṭī.

67 From amongst those who have disqualified this narration are Imām Nawawī, Imām Dāruquṭnī, Imām Dhahabī, Imām Qurṭubī, and others.

This issue—like many other subsidiary issues in the religion—are from those matters that people become very emotional and even fanatical about. Whereas, the reality of the matter is that this is not something that validates or invalidates a person's belief; nor does it cause a person to fall into heresy or deviation. This is because there is no explicitly conclusive evidence for the argument on either side. Hence, the scholars adopted whichever view that they felt was the most correct according to their *ijtihad*[68] based upon the knowledge that Allah had bestowed upon them. The attitude of a believer regarding issues that the scholars differ about should simply be to resign the affair to Allah, and accept that there are many matters which are only known to Him. Observing silence in such cases is the safest path; and Allah knows best.

The best of what has been said in this regard is the statement of ʿAllāma Sayyid Muḥammad Amīn ibn ʿĀbidīn al-Ḥanafī al-Shāmī who said:

> To sum things up—as some of the research scholars have said—it is not appropriate to discuss this issue except with the utmost respect. Also, it is not from those issues regarding which ignorance will be harmful to one's faith, nor will it be asked about in the grave or

68 The furthest extent of deductive reasoning based on Islamic legal maxims. Utilizied by Islamic jurists in the absence of explicit textual evidence.

at the station of reckoning. Therefore, guarding one's tongue regarding it is best.[69]

The lesson to take from this ḥadīth is that despite being much older in age, the Messenger of Allah ﷺ still remembered his mother with a very tender heart, and cried. He suffered the loss of his father and mother at a very young age, yet he did not become bitter, ill-mannered, or harbor hatred for the world. He neither blamed his losses upon anyone nor did he consider himself to be a victim. Rather, despite his tremendous losses during childhood, he became the leader of all humanity. When we ponder over this reality, we will come to the conclusion that such a thing could only have happened through the divine plan of an All-Wise, Almighty Creator, and Majestic Planner. Even the life of the Messenger ﷺ is a sign of Allah's existence and divine guidance. Furthermore, there is a hidden struggle here in the test of the Messenger of Allah ﷺ being prevented from making *istighfār* at this time. This was the state of patience he was required to go through by accepting Allah's decree regarding his parents. Allah ﷻ tested him with their early loss, then later again with the continued grief of their absence, and then with being pleased with the decree of Allah regarding their state.

---

69 *Radd al-Muḥtār*

If we suffer the loss of our elders and loved ones, we should reflect upon the example of our beloved Messenger ﷺ. Along with shouldering all the responsibilities of the world, he was also tested with severe grief.

وفاة عمّه ابي طالب بن عبد المطّلب على ملة قومه وشدة حزنه ﷺ على ذٰلك

The Passing of His Uncle Abū Ṭālib ibn ʿAbd al-Muṭṭalib upon the Religion of His People, and the Severity of His ﷺ Grief over That

Ḥadīth 48

عَنْ سَعِيدُ بْنُ الْمُسَيَّبِ، عَنْ أَبِيهِ، قَالَ لَمَّا حَضَرَتْ أَبَا طَالِبٍ الْوَفَاةُ جَاءَهُ رَسُولُ اللّٰهِ ﷺ فَوَجَدَ عِنْدَهُ أَبَا جَهْلٍ وَعَبْدَ اللّٰهِ بْنَ أَبِي أُمَيَّةَ بْنِ الْمُغِيرَةِ، فَقَالَ أَىْ عَمِّ قُلْ لَا إِلَهَ إِلاَّ اللّٰهُ، كَلِمَةً أُحَاجُّ لَكَ بِهَا عِنْدَ اللّٰهِ. فَقَالَ أَبُو جَهْلٍ وَعَبْدُ اللّٰهِ بْنُ أَبِي أُمَيَّةَ أَتَرْغَبُ عَنْ مِلَّةِ عَبْدِ الْمُطَّلِبِ فَلَمْ يَزَلْ رَسُولُ اللّٰهِ ﷺ يَعْرِضُهَا عَلَيْهِ، وَيُعِيدَانِهِ بِتِلْكَ الْمَقَالَةِ حَتَّى قَالَ أَبُو طَالِبٍ آخِرَ مَا كَلَّمَهُمْ عَلَى مِلَّةِ عَبْدِ الْمُطَّلِبِ، وَأَبَى أَنْ يَقُولَ لَا إِلَهَ إِلاَّ اللّٰهُ. قَالَ: قَالَ رَسُولُ اللّٰهِ ﷺ وَاللّٰهِ لَأَسْتَغْفِرَنَّ لَكَ مَا لَمْ أُنْهَ عَنْكَ. فَأَنْزَلَ اللّٰهُ:

﴿مَا كَانَ لِلنَّبِيِّ وَالَّذِينَ آمَنُوا أَنْ يَسْتَغْفِرُوا لِلْمُشْرِكِينَ﴾ **وَأَنْزَلَ اللهُ فِي أَبِي طَالِبٍ، فَقَالَ لِرَسُولِ اللهِ ﷺ:** ﴿إِنَّكَ لَا تَهْدِي مَنْ أَحْبَبْتَ وَلَكِنَّ اللَّهَ يَهْدِي مَنْ يَشَاءُ﴾

(رواه البخاري)

SAʿĪD IBN AL-MUSAYYIB NARRATES FROM HIS FATHER:

When Abū Ṭālib was on his death bed, the Messenger of Allah ﷺ came to him and found Abū Jahl and ʿAbdullah ibn Abī Umayya ibn al-Mughīra present with him. The Prophet ﷺ said, "O uncle! Say, 'There is no one worthy of worship except Allah,' a statement with which I may intercede on your behalf before Allah." But, Abū Jahl and ʿAbdullah ibn Umayya interrupted, saying, "O Abū Ṭālib! Will you abandon the religion of ʿAbd al-Muṭṭalib?" The Messenger of Allah ﷺ continued urging him to utter the statement of faith, while the others repeated their statement as well, until Abū Ṭālib uttered his final words to them: "Upon the religion of ʿAbd al-Muṭṭalib," refusing to utter, "There is no one worthy of worship except Allah."

The Messenger of Allah ﷺ mentioned, "I swear by Allah, I will definitely seek forgiveness on your behalf, as long as I am not prohibited from doing so." But Allah revealed the verse, "It does not befit the Messenger or those who believe to seek forgiveness for the idolaters."[70] And specifically regarding Abū Ṭālib, He addressed the Messenger of Allah ﷺ revealing the verse, "You cannot guide the one you love, rather Allah will guide whomever He wills."[71]

(Bukhārī)

Commentary

Few things are more difficult upon a believer than to see a loved one refuse the very faith that he has embraced. The Prophet ﷺ faced this test with a person who was quite possibly one of the most beloved people to him. When the Messenger of Allah ﷺ was repeatedly orphaned in childhood—first by the loss of his father, then his mother, then his grandfather—Abū Ṭālib was the one who took him in and raised him as his own. During the early days of Prophethood—at the peak of the Quraysh's persecution—Abū Ṭālib was the one who protected the Prophet ﷺ and defended him from his people. During the boycott, he preferred suffering alongside his nephew, rather than turning him over to his

70 Qur'ān 9:113

71 Qur'ān 28:56

tormentors. Considering all of this we can only begin to imagine the amount of love, appreciation, and compassion that the Messenger of Allah ﷺ had for his dear uncle.

Yet, we see in these final moments, despite the pleading of the Messenger of Allah ﷺ, Abū Ṭālib refuses to leave the religion of his people. The difficulty of being unable to guide the one who had done so much for him, and meant so much to him, was so intense that the Messenger ﷺ had to be consoled by Allah Himself—that guidance is solely in the hands of Allah.

Furthermore, we see the Prophet's desire to supplicate on behalf of his uncle (similar to his desire to supplicate for his mother in the previous ḥadīth), but once again Allah tested him with having patience upon His decree and submitting to His will. Many people find themselves struggling with a similar situation; trying to cope with a loved one who has refused Islam or turned away from it. They may find some consolation knowing that the Prophet ﷺ shared their pain.

استشهاد حِبّهِ زيد بن حارثة ﵁ و حُزْنُهُ عليه ﷺ

The Martyrdom of His Beloved, Zayd Ibn Ḥāritha ﵁, and the Severity of the Prophet's ﷺ Grief over Him

Ḥadīth 49

عَنِ ابْنِ مَسْعُودٍ ﵁ قَالَ: لَمَّا قُتِلَ زَيْدُ بْنُ حَارِثَةَ، أَبْطَأَ أُسَامَةُ عَنِ النَّبِيِّ ﷺ، فَلَمْ يَأْتِهِ، ثُمَّ جَاءَهُ بَعْدَ ذَلِكَ فَقَامَ بَيْنَ يَدَي النَّبِيِّ ﷺ، فَدَمَعَتْ عَيْنَاهُ، فَبَكَى رَسُولُ اللهِ ﷺ فَلَمَّا نَزَفَتْ عَبْرَتُهُ قَالَ النَّبِيُّ ﷺ: لِمَ أَبْطَأْتَ عَنَّا، ثُمَّ جِئْتَ تُحْزِنُنَا؟ قَالَ: فَلَمَّا كَانَ الْغَدُ جَاءَهُ، فَلَمَّا رَآهُ النَّبِيُّ ﷺ مُقْبِلاً قَالَ: إِنِّي لَلاقٍ مِنْكَ الْيَوْمَ مَا لَقِيتُ مِنْكَ أَمْسِ، فَلَمَّا دَنَا دَمَعَتْ عَيْنُهُ فَبَكَى رَسُولُ اللهِ ﷺ.

(رواه عبد الرزاق في مصنّفه)

Ibn Masʿūd ﵁ narrates:

On the day Zayd ibn Ḥāritha was killed, Usāma [the son of Zayd ﵁] had delayed in visiting the Prophet ﷺ, and came to him after some time. As he stood in front of the Prophet ﷺ, his eyes filled with tears. [Seeing this,] the Messenger of Allah ﷺ began to weep. As the tears flowed from his eyes, the Messenger said, "Why did you not come to us earlier? *Now* you come, and remind us of our grief." Ibn Masʿūd ؓ continues, "The next day, Usāma ibn Zayd ؓ came to the Prophet ﷺ. When the Prophet ﷺ saw him approaching he said, "I am seeing from you what I saw from you yesterday." When he drew closer, his eyes filled with tears and the Prophet ﷺ (seeing this) began to weep again.

(ʿAbd al-Razzāq)

Commentary

Zayd ؓ was the adopted son of the Prophet and he loved him like a real son.[72] The loss of Zayd ibn Ḥāritha ؓ was like the loss of a son. So Usāma, the son of Zayd, ؓ was like a grandson to him. Ḥasan, Ḥusayn, and Usāma ؓ would go into the embrace and sit in the lap of the Messenger of

[72] Taking the adopted son as an actual son was later abrogated in Islam. This only applied to the lineage attributed to the child. However, the abrogation did not negate the extremely close relationship that existed between the Prophet ﷺ and Zayd ؓ.

Adopting and raising orphans is one of the greatest of deeds. It is only attributing the adopted child to one's own lineage that is not allowed. As in all matters, those who choose to adopt children should first consult with qualified scholars to properly understand the rulings relating to it.

Allah ﷺ. He would say about Ḥasan and Ḥusayn ‎رضي الله عنهما, "these are my two flowers," and he would refer to Usāma ibn Zayd ‎رضي الله عنه as his "beloved."

This incident shows a very emotional and sentimental state of the Prophet ﷺ and his Companions. At times, such grief would overwhelm them that they would be unable to speak. Loss of wealth, life and loved ones was a part of their everyday existence; as it shall be for all of humanity throughout time. Their trust in Allah, resignation of their affairs to Him, submission to His will, and hope in His reward was what enabled them to remain patient, content, and steadfast despite facing devastating grief.

موت ابنه ابراهيم عليه السلام و شدّة حُزنه ﷺ عليه

THE DEATH OF HIS SON IBRĀHĪM رضي الله عنه AND THE SEVERITY OF HIS ﷺ GRIEF OVER HIM

ḤADĪTH 50

عَنْ أَنَسِ بْنِ مَالِكٍ رضي الله عنه، قَالَ: دَخَلْنَا مَعَ رَسُولِ اللهِ ﷺ عَلَى أَبِي سَيْفٍ القَيْنِ، وَكَانَ ظِئْرًا لِإِبْرَاهِيمَ عَلَيْهِ السَّلاَمُ، فَأَخَذَ رَسُولُ اللهِ ﷺ إِبْرَاهِيمَ، فَقَبَّلَهُ، وَشَمَّهُ، ثُمَّ دَخَلْنَا عَلَيْهِ بَعْدَ ذَلِكَ وَإِبْرَاهِيمُ يَجُودُ بِنَفْسِهِ، فَجَعَلَتْ عَيْنَا رَسُولِ اللهِ ﷺ تَذْرِفَانِ، فَقَالَ لَهُ عَبْدُ الرَّحْمٰنِ بْنُ عَوْفٍ رضي الله عنه: وَأَنْتَ يَا رَسُولَ اللهِ؟ فَقَالَ: يَا ابْنَ عَوْفٍ إِنَّهَا رَحْمَةٌ، ثُمَّ أَتْبَعَهَا بِأُخْرَى، فَقَالَ ﷺ: إِنَّ العَيْنَ تَدْمَعُ، وَالقَلْبَ يَحْزَنُ، وَلاَ نَقُولُ إِلَّا مَا يَرْضَى رَبُّنَا، وَإِنَّا بِفِرَاقِكَ يَا إِبْرَاهِيمُ لَمَحْزُونُونَ.

(رواه البخاري)

ANAS IBN MĀLIK رضي الله عنه NARRATES:

We went with the Messenger of Allah ﷺ to visit the blacksmith Abū Sayf, whose wife was the wet nurse of

Ibrāhīm ؓ (the son of the Prophet ﷺ). The Prophet ﷺ took Ibrāhīm,[73] and he kissed him and smelled him. Later, when we came back, Ibrāhīm was in his last breaths, and the eyes of the Prophet of Allah began to flow with tears. ʿAbd al-Raḥmān ibn ʿAwf asked him, "Even you, O Prophet of Allah?" So he replied, "O Son of ʿAwf, verily this is a mercy." Then he ﷺ wept more and said, "The eye sheds tears and the heart grieves. But we shall not utter anything except that which pleases our Lord. And O Ibrāhīm, we are grieved [by your separation.]"

(Bukhārī)

COMMENTARY

What the heart and eyes do is one thing, and what the hands and tongue do is something else altogether. Tears emanating from the eyes and pain manifesting in the heart are natural occurrences. However, the actions of the tongue and hands (e.g. tearing one's shirt, cursing and yelling profanities, or hitting oneself, etc.) are not natural, and therefore need to be controlled for the sake of Allah. There is neither any shame, nor any negativity associated with the natural responses of the heart. One should be able to express them by letting out one's grief in a healthy manner. The Prophet ﷺ cried, verbally

---

[73] Ibrāhīm ؓ was the youngest of the Prophet's ﷺ children. He passed away in infancy, before he reached two years of age.

expressed his grief without complaint, and mourned together with friends and family. His example was that of balance and perfection even in the most turbulent times of life.

The loss of a child is undoubtedly the greatest tragedy that can afflict a parent; and Allah's Messenger ﷺ was tested by this trial as well. The Prophet's grace, honor, composure, and contentment in Allah's decree manifests itself fully in his ﷺ beautiful response, which is in itself an example for all of mankind.

موت بناته ﷺ حُزنه عليهنّ

The Death of His Daughters and His Grief over Them ﷺ

HADĪTH 51

عَنْ عُرْوَةَ : أَنَّ رَجُلًا أَقْبَلَ بِزَيْنَبَ بِنْتِ رَسُولِ اللهِ ﷺ. فَلَحِقَهُ رَجُلَانِ مِنْ قُرَيْشٍ فَقَاتَلَاهُ حَتَّى غَلَبَاهُ عَلَيْهَا. فَدَفَعَاهَا فَوَقَعَتْ عَلَى صَخْرَةٍ، فَأَسْقَطَتْ وهُرِيقَتْ دَمًا. فَذَهَبُوا بِهَا إِلَى أَبِي سُفْيَانَ، فَجَاءَتْهُ نِسَاءُ بَنِي هَاشِمٍ فَدَفَعَهَا إِلَيْهِنَّ. ثُمَّ جَاءَتْ بَعْدَ ذَلِكَ مُهَاجِرَةً .فَلَمْ تَزَلْ وَجِعَةً حَتَّى مَاتَتْ مِنْ ذَلِكَ الوَجَعِ، فَكَانُوا يَرَوْنَ أَنَّهَا شَهِيدَةٌ.

(رواه الطبراني. قال الهيثمي : رجاله رجال الصحيح)

ᶜUrwa ibn Zubayr narrates:

A man was escorting Zaynab, the daughter of the Messenger of Allah ﷺ [from Makkah to Madīnah]. They were met by two men from the Quraysh, who fought the man accompanying Zaynab until they managed to overpower him and wrest her away from him. The men drove her back, making her fall upon a rock—causing her to bleed and resulting in a miscarriage. So, they then took her to Abū Sufyān. [Hearing the news] the womenfolk of Banū Hāshim[74] came to him, and he handed Zaynab over to them. After that, she was able to migrate and come [to Madīnah]. However, she continued to suffer from her injuries until she died as a result of them. She was thus considered a martyr.

(Ṭabarānī)

ḤADĪTH 52

عَنْ زُهْرِي : تُوُفِّيَتْ رُقَيَّةُ يَوْمَ جَاءَ زَيْدُ بْنُ حَارِثَةَ مَوْلَى رَسُوْلِ اللّٰهِ ﷺ بِبُشْرَى بَدْرٍ.

(رواه الطبراني. قال الهيثمي : مرسل ورجاله ثقات)

ZUHRĪ NARRATES:

Ruqayya (the daughter of the Messenger of Allah ﷺ) passed away on the same day that Zayd ibn Ḥāritha—

[74] The tribe of the Prophet ﷺ.

the freed slave of the Messenger of Allah ﷺ— brought news regarding the victory of Badr.

(Ṭabarānī)

Ḥ
A
D
Ī
T
H
53

عَنْ زُهْرِي : تَزَوَّجَ عُثْمَانُ أُمَّ كُلْثُوْمٍ بِنْتَ رَسُوْلِ اللهِ ﷺ، فتُوُفِّيَتْ عِنْدَهُ وَلَمْ تَلِدْ لَهُ شَيْئًا.

(رواه الطبراني. قال الهيثمي : مرسل ورجاله ثقات)

ZUHRĪ NARRATES:

Uthmān married Umm Kulthūm, the daughter of the Messenger of Allah ﷺ. However, she passed away in his marriage without bearing any children.

(Ṭabarānī)

HADĪTH 54

عَنْ أَنَسِ بْنِ مَالِكٍ رضي الله عنه قَالَ : شَهِدْنَا بِنْتَ رَسُوْلِ اللهِ ﷺ، وَرَسُوْلُ اللهِ ﷺ جَالِسٌ عَلَى الْقَبْرِ، فَرَأَيْتُ عَيْنَاهُ تَدْمَعَانِ ...

(رواه البخاري)

Anas رضي الله عنه narrates:

> We were present at [the funeral of] the daughter of the Messenger of Allah ﷺ. The Messenger of Allah ﷺ was sitting before her grave, and I saw his eyes flowing with tears…

(Bukhārī)

Commentary

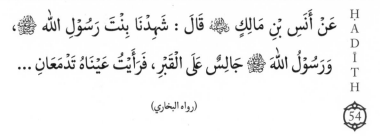

There are few things harder upon a person than having to deal with the death of a child; the mere thought of which is enough to send a shudder down the spine of any parent. Now imagine how the Messenger of Allah ﷺ lived through the death of every single one of his children besides Fāṭima, who was destined to leave this world only six months after the Prophet ﷺ. His immense patience and incredible composure concealed the anguish he faced through these ordeals; the only sign of the ocean of grief within him being the tears that would flow from his eyes.

Every person must face the loss of a loved one at some point in their life. In these moments let us find our patience and composure by taking lesson from the example of our beloved Messenger. May he be enveloped in the peace and blessings of Allah!

موت أحد أحفاده و حُزنه ﷺ عليه

The Death of One of His Grandchildren and His ﷺ Grief over Him

Ḥadīth 55

عَنْ أُسَامَةَ بْنِ زَيْدٍ رضي الله عنهما، قَالَ: كُنَّا عِنْدَ النَّبِيِّ ﷺ إِذْ جَاءَهُ رَسُولُ إِحْدَى بَنَاتِهِ، تَدْعُوهُ إِلَى ابْنِهَا فِي المَوْتِ، فَقَالَ النَّبِيُّ ﷺ: ارْجِعْ إِلَيْهَا فَأَخْبِرْهَا أَنَّ لِلَّهِ مَا أَخَذَ وَلَهُ مَا أَعْطَى، وَكُلُّ شَيْءٍ عِنْدَهُ بِأَجَلٍ مُسَمًّى، فَمُرْهَا فَلْتَصْبِرْ وَلْتَحْتَسِبْ، فَأَعَادَتِ الرَّسُولَ أَنَّهَا قَدْ أَقْسَمَتْ لَتَأْتِيَنَّهَا، فَقَامَ النَّبِيُّ ﷺ وَقَامَ مَعَهُ سَعْدُ بْنُ عُبَادَةَ، وَمُعَاذُ بْنُ جَبَلٍ، فَدُفِعَ الصَّبِيُّ إِلَيْهِ وَنَفْسُهُ تَقَعْقَعُ كَأَنَّهَا فِي شَنٍّ، فَفَاضَتْ عَيْنَاهُ، فَقَالَ لَهُ سَعْدٌ: يَا رَسُولَ اللهِ، مَا هَذَا؟ قَالَ: هَذِهِ رَحْمَةٌ جَعَلَهَا اللهُ فِي قُلُوبِ عِبَادِهِ، وَإِنَّمَا يَرْحَمُ اللهُ مِنْ عِبَادِهِ الرُّحَمَاءَ.

(رواه البخاري)

Usāma ibn Zayd narrates that:

We were with the Prophet ﷺ when a messenger came from one of his daughters, calling him to her son who was dying. The Prophet ﷺ said, "Go back and inform her that to Allah belongs whatever He takes and whatever He gives, and everything has an appointed time with Him. Tell her to have patience and hope for the reward from Allah." But she sent for the Prophet again, swearing that he must come to her. So, the Prophet ﷺ rose [from the gathering], and with him stood Saʿd ibn ʿUbāda and Muʿādh ibn Jabal. When the child was brought to him, he was wheezing and gasping for air. The eyes of the Prophet filled with tears and Saʿd said to him, "O Messenger of Allah, what is this?" He replied, "This is a mercy which Allah has placed in the hearts of His slaves; and Allah only has mercy upon those among His slaves who are merciful."

(Bukhārī)

COMMENTARY

The Arabs of pre-Islamic Arabia were a tough people who considered it unmanly and a sign of weakness to cry at the sight of suffering. At this juncture where the Messenger of Allah ﷺ holds his dying grandson in his arms, similar to the previous ḥadīth, he sheds tears and explains that sympathy and compassion for the weak and suffering is not a sign of weakness but a sign of mercy. And Allah shows mercy to those of His slaves who are merciful to others.

صبره عند عشرة نساءه واعتزاله ﷺ منهن

His Patience in His Domestic Life and His Temporary Separation from His Wives ﷺ

Ḥadīth 56

عَنْ عَبْدِ اللهِ بْنِ عَبَّاسٍ رضي الله عنهما عَنْ عُمَرَ بْنِ الخَطَّابِ رضي الله عنه قَالَ:... كُنَّا مَعْشَرَ قُرَيْشٍ نَغْلِبُ النِّسَاءَ، فَلَمَّا قَدِمْنَا عَلَى الأَنْصَارِ إِذَا قَوْمٌ تَغْلِبُهُمْ نِسَاؤُهُمْ، فَطَفِقَ نِسَاؤُنَا يَأْخُذْنَ مِنْ أَدَبِ نِسَاءِ الأَنْصَارِ، فَصَخِبْتُ عَلَى امْرَأَتِي فَرَاجَعَتْنِي، فَأَنْكَرْتُ أَنْ تُرَاجِعَنِي، قَالَتْ: وَلِمَ تُنْكِرُ أَنْ أُرَاجِعَكَ، فَوَاللهِ إِنَّ أَزْوَاجَ النَّبِيِّ ﷺ لَيُرَاجِعْنَهُ، وَإِنَّ إِحْدَاهُنَّ لَتَهْجُرُهُ اليَوْمَ حَتَّى اللَّيْلِ، فَأَفْزَعَنِي ذَلِكَ وَقُلْتُ لَهَا: قَدْ خَابَ مَنْ فَعَلَ ذَلِكَ مِنْهُنَّ، ثُمَّ جَمَعْتُ عَلَيَّ ثِيَابِي، فَنَزَلْتُ فَدَخَلْتُ عَلَى حَفْصَةَ فَقُلْتُ لَهَا: أَيْ حَفْصَةُ، أَتُغَاضِبُ إِحْدَاكُنَّ النَّبِيَّ ﷺ اليومَ حَتَّى اللَّيْلِ؟ قَالَتْ: نَعَمْ. فَقُلْتُ: قَدْ خِبْتِ وخَسِرْتِ،

أَفَتَأْمَنِينَ أَنْ يَغْضَبَ اللهُ لِغَضَبِ رَسُوْلِهِ ﷺ فَتَهْلِكِي؟ لَا تَسْتَكْثِرِي النَّبِيَّ ﷺ وَلَا تُرَاجِعِيْهِ فِيْ شَيْءٍ وَلَا تَهْجُرِيْهِ...

ʿABDULLĀH IBN ʿABBĀS ﷺ NARRATES FROM ʿUMAR IBN AL-KHAṬṬĀB ﷺ:

...We, the people of Quraysh, prevailed over our women. But when we came to the Anṣār [of Madīnah, we found] a people whose women prevailed over them. Our women quickly took from the mannerisms of the Anṣārī women. [One day], I angrily reprimanded my wife, and she talked back to me. I criticized her for squabbling with me, so she replied, "Don't reproach me for disputing with you. By Allah, even the wives of the Prophet ﷺ speak back to him. One of them even remains aloof from him for the entire day—all the way until the night." [Hearing] this startled me, so I said, "Whoever amongst them does that has failed."

Shortly therafter, I changed my clothes, and went to see Ḥafṣa.[75] I asked her, "O Ḥafṣa, do any of you spend the day with the Prophet ﷺ, upset at each other?" She replied, "Yes." I said to her, "You have failed and perished. Do you feel safe from the wrath of Allah—because of the anger of His Messenger ﷺ—due to which you

[75] The daughter of ʿUmar, and one of the wives of the Prophet ﷺ.

will be destroyed? Do not ask the Prophet ﷺ to give you more; do not argue with him over anything; and do not be aloof from him."…

...فَصَلَّيْتُ صَلَاةَ الفَجْرِ مَعَ النَّبِيِّ ﷺ، فَدَخَلَ النَّبِيُّ ﷺ مَشْرُبَةً لَهُ فَاعْتَزَلَ فِيهَا، وَدَخَلْتُ عَلَى حَفْصَةَ فَإِذَا هِيَ تَبْكِي، فَقُلْتُ: مَا يُبْكِيكِ؟ أَلَمْ أَكُنْ حَذَّرْتُكِ هَذَا؟ أَطَلَّقَكُنَّ النَّبِيُّ ﷺ؟ قَالَتْ: لَا أَدْرِي، هَاهُوَ ذَا مُعْتَزِلٌ فِي الْمَشْرُبَةِ...

…I prayed the *fajr* prayer with the Prophet ﷺ, [immediately] thereafter the Prophet ﷺ entered into one of his upper rooms and secluded himself therein. I came to Ḥafṣa, and found her weeping. I asked her, "What is making you cry? Didn't I warn you about this? Did the Prophet ﷺ divorce all of you?" She replied, "I don't know. He is there in the upper room, secluded."…

...فَدَخَلْتُ عَلَى رَسُولِ اللهِ ﷺ فَإِذَا هُوَ مُضْطَجِعٌ عَلَى رِمَالِ حَصِيرٍ، لَيْسَ بَيْنَهُ وَبَيْنَه فِرَاشٌ، قَدْ أَثَّرَ الرِّمَالُ بِجَنْبِهِ، مُتَّكِئٌ عَلَى وِسَادَةٍ مِنْ أَدَمٍ حَشْوُهَا لِيفٌ، فَسَلَّمْتُ عَلَيْهِ ثُمَّ قُلْتُ وَأَنَا

قَائِمٌ: يَا رَسُوْلَ اللهِ، أَطَلَّقْتَ نِسَاءَكَ؟ فَرَفَعَ إِلَيَّ بَصَرَهُ فَقَالَ: لَا. فَقُلْتُ: اَللهُ أَكْبَرُ، ثُمَّ قُلْتُ وَأَنَا قَائِمٌ أَسْتَأْنِسُ: يَا رَسُوْلَ اللهِ، لَوْ رَأَيْتَنِيْ وَكُنَّا مَعْشَرَ قُرَيْشٍ نَغْلِبُ النِّسَاءَ، فَلَمَّا قَدِمْنَا المَدِيْنَةَ إِذَا قَوْمٌ تَغْلِبُهُمْ نِسَاؤُهُمْ، فَتَبَسَّمَ النَّبِيُّ ﷺ، ثُمَّ قُلْتُ: يَا رَسُوْلَ اللهِ، لَوْ رَأَيْتَنِيْ وَدَخَلْتُ عَلَى حَفْصَةَ فَقُلْتُ لَهَا: وَلَا يَغُرَّنَّكِ أَنْ كَانَتْ جَارَتُكِ أَوْضَأَ مِنْكِ وَأَحَبَّ إِلَى النَّبِيِّ ﷺ. يُرِيْدُ عَائِشَةَ. فَتَبَسَّمَ النَّبِيُّ ﷺ تَبَسُّمَةً أُخْرَى، فَجَلَسْتُ حِيْنَ رَأَيْتُهُ تَبَسَّمَ، فَرَفَعْتُ بَصَرِيْ فِيْ بَيْتِهِ، فَوَاللهِ مَا رَأَيْتُ فِيْ بَيْتِهِ شَيْئًا يَرُدُّ البَصَرَ، غَيْرَ أَهَبَةٍ ثَلَاثٍ، فَقُلْتُ: يَا رَسُوْلَ اللهِ، ٱدْعُ اللهَ فَلْيُوَسِّعْ عَلَى أُمَّتِكَ، فَإِنَّ فَارِسَ والرُّوْمَ قَدْ وُسِّعَ عَلَيْهِمْ وَأُعْطُوا الدُّنْيَا، وَهُمْ لَا يَعْبُدُوْنَ اللهَ. فَجَلَسَ النَّبِيُّ ﷺ وَكَانَ مُتَّكِئًا فَقَالَ: أَوَ فِيْ هَذَا أَنْتَ يَا ابْنَ الْخَطَّابِ! إِنَّ أُولَئِكَ قَوْمٌ عُجِّلُوْا طَيِّبَاتِهِمْ فِيْ الْحَيَاةِ الدُّنْيَا. فَقُلْتُ: يَا رَسُوْلَ اللهِ ٱسْتَغْفِرْ لِيْ...

...I entered the room of the Messenger of Allah ﷺ, and found him lying upon a bare mat [made] of woven fiber, without anything spread between him and the mat[76]—thus the weave [of the mat] left an imprint on his side. He was reclining on a leather pillow stuffed with palm fiber. I greeted him with '*Salām*' and, while still standing, asked, "O Messenger of Allah, have you divorced your wives?" He looked up at me and replied, "No." I said [out of relief], "Allah is the Greatest." Continuing to stand, I sought to open up the discussion and said, "O Messenger of Allah—if you deem it appropriate for me [to speak]—we, the men of Quraysh, prevailed over our women. But when we arrived in Madīnah, we found a people whose women prevailed over them." The Prophet ﷺ smiled. So I continued and said, "O Messenger of Allah—if you deem it appropriate for me [to speak]—I went to Ḥafṣa and said to her, 'Do not be deluded. Your neighbor is more beautiful than you, and more beloved to the Prophet ﷺ.'" (Intending ʿĀʾisha.) The Prophet ﷺ smiled once more. And when I noticed he was smiling, I sat down. I glanced up [and took a look] at his house, and, by Allah, I did not see anything in his house besides three untanned hides. So I said, "O Messenger of Allah, make duʿāʾ so that He may increase the wealth of your Ummah, because the wealth of the Persians and the Romans has been increased. They have been given [the enjoyment of]

[76] To cushion him from the roughness of mat.

this world, whereas they do not worship Allah." The Prophet ﷺ was reclining, but [upon hearing this] he sat up and said, "Are you still of this [mentality], O Son of Khaṭṭāb?! Indeed, they are a people whose blessings have been hastened to them in the life of this world."[77] I [recanted and] said, "O Messenger of Allah, please forgive me."...

...فَاعْتَزَلَ النَّبِيُّ ﷺ نِسَاءَهُ مِنْ أَجْلِ ذَلِكَ الْحَدِيثِ حِينَ أَفْشَتْهُ حَفْصَةُ إِلَى عَائِشَةَ تِسْعًا وَعِشْرِينَ لَيْلَةً، وَكَانَ قَالَ: مَا أَنَا بِدَاخِلٍ عَلَيْهِنَّ شَهْرًا. مِنْ شِدَّةِ مَوْجِدَتِهِ عَلَيْهِنَّ حِينَ عَاتَبَهُ اللهُ، فَلَمَّا مَضَتْ تِسْعٌ وَعِشْرُونَ لَيْلَةً دَخَلَ عَلَى عَائِشَةَ فَبَدَأَ بِهَا،... قَالَتْ عَائِشَةُ: ثُمَّ أَنْزَلَ اللهُ تَعَالَى آيَةَ التَّخْيِيرِ، فَبَدَأَ بِي أَوَّلَ امْرَأَةٍ مِنْ نِسَائِهِ فَاخْتَرْتُهُ، ثُمَّ خَيَّرَ نِسَاءَهُ كُلَّهُنَّ فَقُلْنَ مِثْلَ مَا قَالَتْ عَائِشَةُ.

(رواه البخاري)

...The Prophet ﷺ remained secluded from his wives for twenty-nine days during this incident, when Ḥafṣa had

---

77 Leaving them with nothing for the Hereafter.

divulged [a private matter] of the Prophet ﷺ to ʿĀʾisha. He had said, "I will not go to them for a month," due to the extent of his displeasure towards them, until Allah addressed him [in the matter]. When twenty-nine nights had passed, he entered ʿĀʾisha's room and began [giving each of his wives a choice], starting with her...

ʿĀʾisha explained, "Allah the Exalted revealed the verse of "Giving Choice."[78] So, the Messenger of Allah ﷺ began with me, giving me the choice first out of his wives. I chose to remain with him."

Thereafter, he gave each of his wives the choice, and they all said the same thing as ʿĀʾisha.

(Bukhārī)

Commentary

This ḥadīth gives us a glimpse into the family life of the Prophet ﷺ. It gives us insight into how much the Prophet ﷺ shared in the life experiences of regular people. Due to his

---

78 "O Prophet, tell your wives, 'If your desire is for the present life and its finery, then come, I will make provision for you and release you with kindness. But if you desire Allah, His Messenger, and the Final Abode, then remember that Allah has prepared great rewards for those of you who do good." (Qurʾān 33:28-29)

lofty status as the Messenger of Allah ﷺ, one might envision that he had a blissfully sublime marital life, totally devoid of any arguments, difficulties, or challenges. However, this narration shows that the Messenger ﷺ went through many of these issues, like everyone else.

Qāḍī ʿIyāḍ writes, "Someone able to marry and carry out the obligations incurred by marriage without being distracted from his Lord has a lofty degree. Such is the degree of our Prophet ﷺ—having many wives did not distract him from worshipping his Lord. Indeed, it increased him in worship, in that he protected his wives, gave them their rights, earned for them, and guided them."[79]

The Prophet ﷺ is the most honored of Allah's creation, and his wives are the honored "mothers of the believers."[80] Someone may ask, how can the wives of the Messenger ﷺ possibly argue with him, or have the boldness to speak to him in this way? To answer this question, we must first correct this notion; the Messenger of Allah ﷺ and his noble wives were still human. As was mentioned in the previous chapters, the belief of Ahl al-Sunnah wal-Jamāʿah is that anything related to normal human experience can also be faced by a

79 *Al-Shifā*

80 Qurʾān 33:6

prophet. Therefore, it is normal for them and their families to experience worldly problems, sadness, grief, or any other human condition.

One of the divine wisdoms in Allah allowing these incidents to occur, and for the Ṣaḥābah to narrate these stories, is that it allows us—the followers of the Messenger—to learn how to deal with these situations. In this way we can follow his example in how he treated his wives and responded to their attitudes whenever we face any conflict with our own spouses.

The background of this incident is that some spoils of war came in from one of the battles. The entire family of the Prophet ﷺ lived an ascetic life, as we have discussed in some of the previous ḥadīths. The wives thought they may be rightfully entitled to receive a portion of this wealth because of the struggles they ordinarily faced. Their asking for an increase in the Prophet's expenditure upon them was not a demand for the luxuries of this world, rather it was a request to come out of the hardship they faced on a daily basis. They made a mistake in judgement by persisting in the expectation that they receive something, leading to the displeasure of the Prophet ﷺ due to their insistence upon a worldly matter. For the honor of being wed to the most Beloved of Allah's creation, Allah demanded from them a higher standard, and revealed:

﴿يَا أَيُّهَا النَّبِيُّ قُل لِّأَزْوَاجِكَ إِن كُنتُنَّ تُرِدْنَ الْحَيَاةَ الدُّنْيَا وَزِينَتَهَا
فَتَعَالَيْنَ أُمَتِّعْكُنَّ وَأُسَرِّحْكُنَّ سَرَاحًا جَمِيلًا ۞ وَإِن كُنتُنَّ تُرِدْنَ اللَّهَ
وَرَسُولَهُ وَالدَّارَ الْآخِرَةَ فَإِنَّ اللَّهَ أَعَدَّ لِلْمُحْسِنَاتِ مِنكُنَّ أَجْرًا عَظِيمًا﴾

"O Prophet, say to your wives, 'If your desire is for the present life and its finery, then come, I will make provision for you and release you with kindness, but if you desire Allah, His Messenger, and the Final Abode, then remember that Allah has prepared great rewards for those of you who do good."

(Qur'ān 33:28-29)

Of course, once this became clear to them, they all took heed and preferred Allah and His Messenger over all else. This was the great patience that was demanded on their part to remain in marriage with the Messenger ﷺ.

Many men and women encounter some form of difficulty in their marriage. However, if they were to recognize that their marriage is a means of devotion and drawing closer to Allah, it would help them tolerate such difficulty with greater patience as well as help them see that such patience serves the purpose of pleasing one's Lord. And Allah says:

﴿فَإِنَّ مَعَ الْعُسْرِ يُسْرًا ۞ إِنَّ مَعَ الْعُسْرِ يُسْرًا ﴾

So, undoubtedly, with hardship, there is ease.
Undoubtedly, with hardship, there is ease.

(Qur'ān 94:5-6)

Thus, the secret to a successful marriage is not to be constantly concerned with eliminating conflict, rather it is in learning how to deal with and manage these conflicts when they arise. This starts with each spouse realizing that though their partner may not be perfect, they still possess many excellent qualities that make them beloved. By focusing on their good and being patient with their shortcomings, a person will learn to love their spouse instead of lose love for them on account of them being human. This is best summarized in the words of the Prophet ﷺ recorded in *Saḥīḥ Muslim*:

لاَ يَفْرَكْ مُؤْمِنٌ مُؤْمِنَةً إِنْ كَرِهَ مِنْهَا خُلُقًا رَضِيَ مِنْهَا آخَرَ - أَوْ قَالَ - غَيْرَهُ

"A believing man should never hate a believing woman (i.e. his wife). If he is displeased with something of her character, he will be pleased with something else."

Imām al-Ubbi ﵀ explains, "It is not appropriate for a man to completely despise his wife when he sees something within her that displeases him. Because, even if he is displeased with one thing, he will still be pleased with something else. So, whatever he likes in her ought to compensate for what he dislikes."[81]

Mullā ʿAlī al-Qārī ﵀ further elaborates, "There is an indication in this that there is no spouse that exists who is free from deficiency. Therefore, anyone who desires [a spouse] who is free from flaw will remain spouse-less. People, especially believers, are not free from at least some praiseworthy traits, so it is necessary to consider the good and overlook the rest."[82]

This story of the Messenger ﷺ and his wives is a treasure trove filled with wisdom and lessons to learn from. From this we see the Prophet ﷺ did not revile, insult, curse, or beat his wives when he became displeased with them. He did not physically, emotionally, or verbally abuse them. He continued to fulfill the duty of a husband, and at no point do we see any immoderation or abuse from his side. All he did was stay aloof from them so that they themselves would understand their mistake. That they ultimately did so is clear from the culmination of this ḥadīth, when all the wives chose to remain with the Messenger of Allah ﷺ and prefer him over all else.

---

[81]   *Ikmālu Ikmāli 'l-Muʿlim*

[82]   *Mirqāt al-Mafātīḥ Sharḥ Mishkāt al-Maṣābīḥ*

Taking heed of the example of the Messenger of Allah ﷺ and his wives, and taking note of his advice, should help every one of us in our domestic lives. May Allah make our spouses a coolness for our eyes, and a comfort for our hearts!

HADĪTH 57

عَنْ عُرْوَةَ : أَنَّ رَسُولَ اللهِ ﷺ طَلَّقَ سَوْدَةَ فَلَمَّا خَرَجَ إِلَى الصَّلَاةِ أَمْسَكَتْ بِثَوْبِهِ فَقَالَتْ: مَا لِيَ فِيْ الرِّجَالِ حَاجَةٌ لَكِنِّي أُرِيْدُ أَنْ أُحْشَرَ فِيْ أَزْوَاجِكَ . قَالَ فَرَجَعَهَا وَجَعَلَ يَوْمَهَا لِعَائِشَةَ .

(رواه البيهقي وأخرجه ابن حجر في تلخيص وقال: هو مرسل)

ʿURWA NARRATES:

The Messenger of Allah ﷺ gave Sawda a (single, revocable) divorce. When he was leaving for the prayer, she held him by his garment and said, "I [am not of that age] to be in need [of the company of] a husband. However, I wish to be raised [in the Hereafter] amongst your wives." So, he took her back, and designated her day for ʿĀʾisha.

(Bayhaqī)

Commentary

Imām Ibn al-Humām explains, "The Messenger of Allah ﷺ gave Sawda ﵂ a *single revocable divorce*. In such a case, a complete separation does not occur immediately upon uttering words of divorce, rather it only occurs at the end of its waiting period.[83] [...So in this case, Sawda ﵂ was in the middle of her waiting period,] and she was afraid that her waiting period would end [without the Messenger ﷺ taking her back] thus resulting in her being completely separated from him ﷺ."

There are many reasons for divorce. Though both spouses may faithfully carry out their marital duties and fulfill their partner's rights, marital discord can still develop solely due to lack of compatibility. It is not necessary to label one of the spouses as "the antagonist", to explain why friction develops in a relationship. Thus, it is possible for divorce to occur—with due cause—without any blame falling upon either spouse.

Understanding this, we realize that this incident does not take away from the piety or rank of Sawda ﵂ as one of the Mothers of the Believers. A problem within domestic

---

[83] This is referring to the *ʿiddah*—the waiting period which lasts three menstrual cycles after a divorce is issued, before the divorce is finalized. When a single revocable divorce is issued, a man has the option to take his wife back during the *ʿiddah* without having to renew the marriage.

life may have caused the Prophet ﷺ to issue a divorce to her. However, the Messenger ﷺ did ultimately take her back into his marriage, guaranteeing her the status of being wed to him in Paradise. And as is mentioned in a narration of Bukhārī, she willingly offered her exclusive day with the Prophet ﷺ to ʿĀʾisha ﷺ because she knew that this would please him. This demonstrates that whatever led him to issue the divorce could not have been a fatal flaw in the character of Sawda ﷺ.

Additionally, note the method in which the Prophet ﷺ issued the divorce. He did not issue three divorces at once in a reprehensible way that would completely terminate the marriage and leave no possibility of return. Rather, he issued a single divorce, which was revocable.[84] This gave time for thought, reflection, and—most importantly—reconciliation. Therefore, when Sawda ﷺ desired to return to the Prophet ﷺ, there was an opportunity for him to accept her back. And what better reason to reconcile than to hope for the reward of the afterlife?

There is also an important lesson in this for those dealing with marital conflict. Divorce is a valid option when there is no hope of living in harmony, or when there is severe,

---

[84] For those who are unaware of the Islamic rulings of divorce it is critical to learn them before even considering divorce. Those that pursue a matter in ignorance, will definitely lament its outcome.

irreparable harm being inflicted on either side. Nevertheless, divorce should not be sought in haste. Considering divorce with patience and deliberation can save a couple from a lifetime of sorrow and regret. In one narration the Messenger of Allah ﷺ said:

التَّأَنِّي مِنْ اللهِ وَالْعَجَلَةُ مِنْ الشَّيْطَانِ

"Acting with careful composure is from Allah, and acting in haste is from Shayṭān"

(Bayhaqī and Tirmidhī)

Despite the fact that the Messenger of Allah ﷺ was the most perfect human being to walk the earth, and his wives were also chosen and from the elite of Allah's servants, they still experienced challenges in their domestic life.

His Endurance in Worship & Devotion

صلى الله عليه وآله وسلم

مجاهدته ﷺ في الطاعات و عبادة ربّه

His Striving ﷺ in the Obedience and Worship of His Lord

صفة تهجده ﷺ

The Manner of His Tahajjud

Ḥadīth 58

عَنْ عَائِشَةَ رضي الله عنها: أَنَّ نَبِيَّ اللهِ ﷺ كَانَ يَقُومُ مِنَ اللَّيْلِ حَتَّى تَتَفَطَّرَ قَدَمَاهُ، فَقَالَتْ عَائِشَةُ: لِمَ تَصْنَعُ هَذَا يَا رَسُولَ اللهِ، وَقَدْ غَفَرَ اللهُ لَكَ مَا تَقَدَّمَ مِنْ ذَنْبِكَ وَمَا تَأَخَّرَ؟ قَالَ: أَفَلاَ أُحِبُّ أَنْ أَكُونَ عَبْدًا شَكُورًا؟ فَلَمَّا كَثُرَ لَحْمُهُ صَلَّى جَالِسًا، فَإِذَا أَرَادَ أَنْ يَرْكَعَ قَامَ فَقَرَأَ ثُمَّ رَكَعَ.

(رواه البخاري)

ʿĀʾisha رضي الله عنها narrates:

The Prophet ﷺ would stand in prayer during the night until his feet would swell. ʿĀʾisha رضي الله عنها would ask, "Why do you do this, O Messenger of Allah, when Allah has already forgiven your past and future faults?" He ﷺ replied, "Should I not then be a grateful slave?"

When his blessed body gained weight, he would pray sitting. When he wanted to perform *rukūʿ*, he would stand and recite, then he would bow.

(Bukhārī)

ḤADĪTH 59

عَنْ حُذَيْفَةَ رضي الله عنه، أَنَّهُ رَأَى رَسُولَ اللهِ ﷺ يُصَلِّي مِنَ اللَّيْلِ، فَكَانَ يَقُولُ: اللهُ أَكْبَرُ - ثَلَاثًا - ذُو الْمَلَكُوتِ وَالْجَبَرُوتِ وَالْكِبْرِيَاءِ وَالْعَظَمَةِ، ثُمَّ اسْتَفْتَحَ فَقَرَأَ الْبَقَرَةَ، ثُمَّ رَكَعَ فَكَانَ رُكُوعُهُ نَحْوًا مِنْ قِيَامِهِ، وَكَانَ يَقُولُ فِي رُكُوعِهِ: سُبْحَانَ رَبِّيَ الْعَظِيمِ، سُبْحَانَ رَبِّيَ الْعَظِيمِ، ثُمَّ رَفَعَ رَأْسَهُ مِنَ الرُّكُوعِ، فَكَانَ قِيَامُهُ نَحْوًا مِنْ قِيَامِهِ، يَقُولُ: لِرَبِّيَ الْحَمْدُ، ثُمَّ سَجَدَ، فَكَانَ سُجُودُهُ نَحْوًا مِنْ

قِيَامِهِ، فَكَانَ يَقُولُ فِي سُجُودِهِ: سُبْحَانَ رَبِّيَ الْأَعْلَى، ثُمَّ رَفَعَ رَأْسَهُ مِنَ السُّجُودِ، وَكَانَ يَقْعُدُ فِيمَا بَيْنَ السَّجْدَتَيْنِ نَحْوًا مِنْ سُجُودِهِ، وَكَانَ يَقُولُ: رَبِّ اغْفِرْ لِي، رَبِّ اغْفِرْ لِي، فَصَلَّى أَرْبَعَ رَكَعَاتٍ، فَقَرَأَ فِيهِنَّ الْبَقَرَةَ، وَآلَ عِمْرَانَ، وَالنِّسَاءَ، وَالْمَائِدَةَ، أَوِ الْأَنْعَامَ، شَكَّ شُعْبَةُ.

(رواه أبو داود)

Ḥudhayfa ibn al-Yamān narrates that he saw the Messenger of Allah ﷺ praying in the night:

He was saying, "Allah is the Greatest," thrice, followed by, "[He is] the Possessor of dominion, power, majesty and greatness." He then recited Sūrah al-Fātiḥah and followed it up with Sūrah al-Baqarah. Then he went into *rukū*ʾ[85]—and the length of his *rukū*ʾ was just as long as his standing—and he said in his *rukū*ʾ, "Glorified is my Lord the Greatest." Then he raised his head from *rukū*ʾ —and his standing was just as long as his [initial] standing—as he said, "All praise is due to my Lord." He then went into *sajdah*.[86] His *sajdah* was just as long

85 Bowing

86 Prostration

as his standing, and he recited in his *sajdah*, "Glorified be my Lord, the Most High." Then he raised his head and sat between the two *sajdahs*—and the length of his sitting was just as long as his *sajdah*—and he said, "My Lord, forgive me, my Lord, forgive me." He prayed four *rakaʿahs,* and he read in them Sūrah al-Baqarah, Sūrah Āl Imrān, Sūrah al-Nisāʾ, and either Sūrah al-Māʾidah or Sūrah al-Anʿām.

(Abū Dāwūd)

Commentary

Conversing with the Beloved and engaging in intimate conversation with Him is something that can make a person go into a state of ecstasy. It can engulf an individual to such an extent that they lose track of time and space. We see the ardent love and deep connection that the Messenger of Allah ﷺ had with his Beloved Lord. Up to six *ajzāʾ*[87]—approximately one fifth—of the Qurʾān would be recited in one ṣalāh… Allahu Akbar! Truly this feat can only be accomplished by one who is blessed by Allah's grace and is in such a state of love with his Lord that he does not experience hardship in standing for such long hours.

In our times, if we happen to stand in *tarāwīḥ* prayers a little longer than usual, we start feeling frustrated and sometimes

[87] Plural of *juzʾ*, or a thirtieth of the Qurʾān.

complain about why the Imām is lengthening the prayer so much. If the true love of Allah were to penetrate our hearts, then a few extra minutes of standing would not bother us. The worship of lovers is not merely "getting the job done" the way a person runs an errand; rather, it is an intimate conversation with the Beloved. If we study the life of the Prophet ﷺ, reflect upon it and emulate it, then we will be able to upgrade our worship and raise it to this higher standard.

صفة صومه ﷺ

The Manner of His Fast

HADĪTH 60

عَنْ حُمَيْدٍ، أَنَّهُ سَمِعَ أَنَسًا رضي الله عنه، يَقُولُ: كَانَ رَسُولُ اللهِ ﷺ يُفْطِرُ مِنَ الشَّهْرِ حَتَّى نَظُنَّ أَنْ لاَ يَصُومَ مِنْهُ، وَيَصُومُ حَتَّى نَظُنَّ أَنْ لاَ يُفْطِرَ مِنْهُ شَيْئًا، وَكَانَ لاَ تَشَاءُ أَنْ تَرَاهُ مِنَ اللَّيْلِ مُصَلِّيًا إِلَّا رَأَيْتَهُ، وَلاَ نَائِمًا إِلَّا رَأَيْتَهُ.

(رواه البخاري)

ANAS ؓ NARRATES:

The Messenger of Allah ﷺ [sometimes] would not fast during certain months, to such an extent that we would think that he will not observe the fast at all in that month. And [sometimes] he would [continuously] fast to such an extent that would think he will not omit any day of fasting in that entire month. [His actions were such that] whoever wished to see him performing prayer at night, could do so. And whoever wished to see him sleeping at night, could do so.

(Bukhārī)

ḤADĪTH 61

عَنْ هَمَّامٍ، أَنَّهُ سَمِعَ أَبَا هُرَيْرَةَ رضي الله عنه، عَنِ النَّبِيِّ ﷺ، قَالَ: إِيَّاكُمْ وَالوِصَالَ، مَرَّتَيْنِ، قِيلَ: إِنَّكَ تُوَاصِلُ، قَالَ: إِنِّي أَبِيتُ يُطْعِمُنِي رَبِّي وَيَسْقِينِ، فَاكْلَفُوا مِنَ العَمَلِ مَا تُطِيقُونَ.

(رواه البخاري)

ABŪ HURAYRA 🌸 NARRATES:

> The Messenger of Allah 🌸 said twice, "I caution you from [doing] *wiṣāl*."[88] Someone asked him, "But you observe *wiṣāl?*" He 🌸 replied, "Verily my Lord nourishes me in my sleep. Therefore, take upon yourself of good deeds only that which you are capable of handling."

(Bukhārī)

COMMENTARY

From these ḥadīths we can learn some principles of treading the path to Allah.

First, we must keep training the *nafs* in different ways under the guidance and spiritual training of a qualified shaykh. The Messenger of Allah 🌸 and his Companions had a spiritual regimen of fasting, standing the nights in *tahajjud*, reciting the Qurʾān, remembrance of Allah, and other litanies. We see in these ḥadīths how much hardship the Prophet 🌸 would undergo in his devotion to Allah.

A layman may wonder why someone would put themselves through so much difficulty in worship? However, we can pose the exact same question to those who put themselves

---

88 To continuously fast for two days straight, including the night, without eating anything in between.

through tremendous strain for the sake of worldly gain. After all, many people work so much that they do not see their wife and children for days, weeks, or even months on end. The only reason people tolerate this stress is because they see an inherent benefit in their work. Thus, if accumulating wealth is a good enough reason to tolerate difficulties, then shouldn't earning the pleasure of the Creator of all comfort be a better reason?

We also learn from these ḥadīths that there were certain acts of devotion that were only meant for the Prophet ﷺ. Thus, out of compassion for his Ummah, he forbade them from attempting such worship that entailed a level of physical and spiritual hardship that they would not be able to endure. A normal person cannot possess the physical and spiritual strength of a Prophet, who is perpetually being sustained by Allah.

We also gather from this that a leader and spiritual mentor of a people should have a higher level of devotion and commitment that is above and beyond that of others. This is what sets him apart from the people and puts him at a loftier rank. As Allah ﷻ says:

﴿وَلِكُلٍّ دَرَجَٰتٌ مِّمَّا عَمِلُوا۟ۚ﴾

"And for all are degrees (or ranks) according to their deeds."

(Qur'ān 6:132)

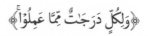

سقوطه ﷺ مِنَ الفَرَس و خَدْشُ جَنْبِهِ

Falling From His ﷺ Horse and Scraping His Side

HADĪTH 62

عَنْ أَنَسِ بْنِ مَالِكٍ رضي الله عنه، قَالَ: سَقَطَ رَسُولُ اللهِ ﷺ مِنْ فَرَسٍ فَخُدِشَ - أَوْ قال: فَجُحِشَ - شِقُّهُ الأَيْمَنُ، فَدَخَلْنَا عَلَيْهِ نَعُودُهُ، فَحَضَرَتِ الصَّلاَةُ، فَصَلَّى قَاعِدًا، فَصَلَّيْنَا قُعُودًا...

(رواه البخاري)

Anas ibn Mālik رضي الله عنه narrates:

The Messenger of Allah ﷺ fell from his horse and scraped or injured his right side. So, we went to visit him and inquired about his health. [When] the time of prayer entered, he prayed sitting down so we [also] prayed sitting down.

(Bukhārī)

Commentary

We see from this ḥadīth that the Messenger of Allah ﷺ experienced mundane difficulties just like others. These everyday accidents and physical injuries that we may think only affect us were also experienced by the Prophet ﷺ. His Lord put him through various difficulties to demonstrate the perfection of his human qualities— such as patience and forbearance—for the entire world to see.

SICKNESS
AND THE FINAL DAYS OF THE
BELOVED PROPHET

صلى الله عليه وآله وسلم

The Severity of His Illness; and His Patience and Anticipation for Its Reward

Hadith 63

عن أبي سعيد الخدري رضي الله عنه أنَّه قال دَخَلْتُ عَلَى النَّبِيِّ ﷺ وَهُوَ يُوعَكُ , فَوَضَعْتُ يَدِي عَلَيْهِ , فَوَجَدْتُ حَرَّهُ بَيْنَ يَدَيَّ فَوْقَ اللِّحَافِ , فَقُلْتُ : يَا رَسُولَ اللهِ , مَا أَشَدَّهَا عَلَيْكَ , قَالَ : إِنَّا كَذَلِكَ يُضَعَّفُ لَنَا الْبَلَاءُ وَيُضَعَّفُ لَنَا الْأَجْرُ. قُلْتُ : يَا رَسُولَ اللهِ , أَيُّ النَّاسِ أَشَدُّ بَلَاءً ؟ قَالَ : الْأَنْبِيَاءُ. قُلْتُ : يَا رَسُولَ اللهِ , ثُمَّ مَنْ ؟ قَالَ : ثُمَّ الصَّالِحُونَ , إِنْ كَانَ أَحَدُهُمْ لَيُبْتَلَى بِالْفَقْرِ حَتَّى مَا يَجِدُ أَحَدُهُمْ إِلَّا الْعَبَاءَةَ يُحَوِّيهَا , وَإِنْ كَانَ أَحَدُهُمْ لَيَفْرَحُ بِالْبَلَاءِ كَمَا يَفْرَحُ أَحَدُكُمْ بِالرَّخَاءِ.

(رواه ابن ماجة و قال البوصيري في الزوائد: اسناده صحيح و رجاله ثقات)

Abū Saʿīd al-Khudrī ؓ narrates:

> I visited the Messenger of Allah ﷺ while he was ill. I placed my hand upon him and could feel the [intense] heat of his [fever] through the blanket. I remarked, "Your fever is very severe!" The Messenger of Allah ﷺ replied, "Indeed just as our afflictions are multiplied, our rewards are also multiplied." Then I asked, "O Messenger of Allah, who are the most tested amongst mankind?" He ﷺ replied, "The Prophets." I continued, "Then who?" He ﷺ replied, "The righteous. Some of them are afflicted with poverty to such an extent that they do not find anything to wear except a single woolen sheet that they wrap around their body. Each one of them is just as delighted with their trial as any of you are with ease and comfort."

(Ibn Mājah).

Commentary

This ḥadīth completely opposes the general notion most people have of the relationship between Allah and His closest servants. Most people assume Allah makes things easy—that He removes tests and obstacles—for those whom He loves. However, true devotion and love does not manifest in times of ease and comfort. Rather, true love and devotion become apparent when comfort is taken away and one finds nothing but hardship. For this reason, the most beloved of Allah's slaves are not those who merely love His blessings and bounties; instead they are those who love the very Being of Allah. *They love Allah simply because He is their Lord,* not because of His bestowals, blessings, bounties or favors. Their love for Allah is unconditional, unwavering. Furthermore, *Allah loves them* and has selected them especially for Himself.

The People of Allah are His proof before all of creation. They are a proof of the internal and external resilience that He has bestowed upon humankind. They are a proof that the capacity that He bestowed upon the Children of Ādam is truly worthy of the honor of being prostrated to by the angels. It is, in essence, the response to the angels when they asked Allah, "Will You create something that shall cause corruption and shed blood?"[89] If someone asks, "If Allah loves them so much, then why does He allow them to be hurt?" It is because in lieu of this temporary and short-lived pain, Allah, the Exalted, wishes to bestow upon them everlasting and eternal bliss.

It has been narrated by Anas ibn Mālik ﵁ that the Messenger of Allah ﷺ said, "The most well-to-do and blissful person (of this world) will be brought forth on the Day of Judgment and immersed, for an instant, into Jahannam.[90] He will then

89 Qur'ān 2:30

90 Hellfire

be asked, 'O son of Adam, did you ever see a day of good? Did you ever see any enjoyment?' to which he will reply, 'By Allah! No, my Lord.' Then the most miserable and distressed person of this world will be brought forth and immersed, for an instant, into Jannah.[91] He will then be asked, 'Did you ever see a day of misery? Did you ever experience any hardship?' to which he will reply, 'No, by Allah! My Lord, never did I suffer misery nor did I see a day of hardship!'"[92]

The eternal bounties, blessings and enjoyment of Paradise literally dissolve all worldly ordeals into nothing. Compared with Allah's eternal pleasure and divine love, the struggles of this life are a very cheap price to pay.

---

91 Paradise

92 Aḥmad and Muslim

حالة الفقر الّتي مات عليها سيّد ولد آدم
صلوات الله عليه و سلامه

The State of Poverty In Which the Leader of Humankind Died—Peace and Blessings of Allah be upon Him

Ḥadīth 64

عَنْ أَبِي بُرْدَةَ بْنِ أَبِي مُوسَى الْأَشْعَرِيِّ ﵁ قَالَ: دَخَلْتُ عَلَى عَائِشَةَ، فَأَخْرَجَتْ إِلَيْنَا إِزَارًا غَلِيظًا مِمَّا يُصْنَعُ بِالْيَمَنِ، وَكِسَاءً مِنَ الَّتِي يُسَمُّونَهَا الْمُلَبَّدَةَ، قَالَ: فَأَقْسَمَتْ بِاللهِ إِنَّ رَسُولَ اللهِ ﷺ قُبِضَ فِي هَذَيْنِ الثَّوْبَيْنِ.

(رواه مسلم)

Abū Burda ibn Abū Mūsā al-Ashʿarī ﵁ narrates:

I visited ʿĀʾisha, so she took out a thick Yemeni *izār*[93] and another garment made from something called

---

[93] A lower garment that is wrapped around the body.

mulabbadah.[94] She then took an oath by Allah that, indeed, the Messenger of Allah ﷺ passed away in theses two [simple] garments.

(Muslim)

Commentary

The thick cloth that the Messenger of Allah ﷺ had on him when he passed away was a rough, inexpensive, and simple cloth. It was not the preferred material to wear in the hot climate of Arabia. We see the ultimate humility of a man who—despite conquering all of Arabia, including hearts and minds, in his very lifetime—chose to live in austerity. The humble garment of this humble man—may the peace and blessings of Allah be upon him—was a clear indication of his abstinence from the pleasures and comforts of this ephemeral world, due to his direct connection to the Lord of All the Worlds.

[94] A type of thick cloth which gives the appearance of having two layers.

مجاهدته ﷺ عند سكرات الموت و شوقه للقاء ربّه

His ﷺ Struggle During the Pangs of Death and His Longing to Meet His Lord

Ḥadīth 65

عَنْ أَبِي عَمْرٍو ذَكْوَانَ، مَوْلَى عَائِشَةَ: أَنَّ عَائِشَةَ، رَضِيَ اللهُ عَنْهَا، كَانَتْ تَقُولُ: إِنَّ رَسُولَ اللهِ ﷺ كَانَ بَيْنَ يَدَيْهِ رَكْوَةٌ - أَوْ قَالَ: عُلْبَةٌ فِيهَا مَاءٌ، يَشُكُّ عُمَرُ - فَجَعَلَ يُدْخِلُ يَدَيْهِ فِي الْمَاءِ، فَيَمْسَحُ بِهِمَا وَجْهَهُ، وَيَقُولُ: لاَ إِلَهَ إِلاَّ اللهُ، إِنَّ لِلْمَوْتِ سَكَرَاتٍ، ثُمَّ نَصَبَ يَدَهُ فَجَعَلَ يَقُولُ: فِي الرَّفِيقِ الأَعْلَى، حَتَّى قُبِضَ وَمَالَتْ يَدُهُ.

(رواه البخاري)

Abū ʿAmr Dhakwān narrates that ʿĀ'isha ﷺ would mention:

"The Messenger of Allah ﷺ had a small container of water, made of leather or wood,[95] that was with him [when he was on his deathbed]. He would put his hand into the water and wipe his face with it while saying, "There is none worthy of worship but Allah.

---

95 ʿUmar ibn Saʿīd, the narrator, was not sure if it was made of leather or wood.

Verily, the pangs of death are severe." Then he lifted his hands, and began saying, "[O Allah, let me be] with the Highest Companion."[96] Until he passed away and his hand slumped down.

(Bukhārī)

Commentary

Our beloved Prophet ﷺ was born into hardship, endured a life of hardship, and ended his life in hardship—may Allah bless him and grant him eternal peace. After all this hardship and difficulty, we see his state in the final moments of his life; supplicating his Lord with the most sublime duʿāʾ, wherein he ﷺ asks to be united with his True Beloved… and he is then called back.

We ask Allah, out of the love we have in our hearts for Him and His Messenger ﷺ, to join us with Him and His beloveds when we also pass away from this world. *Āmīn*!

96 Referring to Allah Himself.

Conclusion

أشدّ البلاء يأتي على أصلب الناس ديناً و ثواب البلاء

THE SEVEREST AFFLICTIONS COME UPON THE ONE WHO IS THE STRONGEST IN RELIGION, AND THE REWARDS OF THOSE AFFLICTIONS

عن سَعْدِ بْنِ أَبِي وَقَّاصٍ ﷺ قَالَ: قُلْتُ: يَا رَسُولَ اللهِ، أَيُّ النَّاسِ أَشَدُّ بَلاَءً؟ قَالَ: الأَنْبِيَاءُ ثُمَّ الأَمْثَلُ فَالأَمْثَلُ، فَيُبْتَلَى الرَّجُلُ عَلَى حَسَبِ دِينِهِ، فَإِنْ كَانَ دِينُهُ صُلْبًا اشْتَدَّ بَلاَؤُهُ، وَإِنْ كَانَ فِي دِينِهِ رِقَّةٌ ابْتُلِيَ عَلَى حَسَبِ دِينِهِ، فَمَا يَبْرَحُ البَلاَءُ بِالعَبْدِ حَتَّى يَتْرُكَهُ يَمْشِي عَلَى الأَرْضِ مَا عَلَيْهِ خَطِيئَةٌ.

(رواه الترمذيّ).

SAʿD IBN ABĪ WAQQĀS NARRATES:

I once asked, "O Messenger of Allah, who amongst mankind are the most severely afflicted?" He replied, "The prophets, then those nearest to them, and then those nearest to them. A man will be tested according

> to the level of his piety. Therefore, if he is firm in his religion, then his tribulations will be more severe; and if he is weak in his religion then he will be tested according to the level of his religion. The slave of Allah will continue to face afflictions until they leave him walking upon the Earth sinless."

(Tirmidhī)

COMMENTARY

We see from this ḥadīth that trial and affliction are nothing but mercy and purification from sins for the slaves of Allah. We also learn that the severest trials will only come upon those whose faith and devotion to Allah is most firm. For this reason, people of weak faith become bitter, angry, and frustrated when they are tested through afflictions. Whereas those who have a stronger link with Allah continue to exhibit patience, contentment, and gratefulness despite going through difficult circumstances.

الصبر على البلاء و الاحتساب من عطايا الرحمٰن جَلَّ جَلَالُهُ

Having Patience upon Tribulations and Anticipating the Reward from the Bounties of the All Merciful جَلَّ جَلَالُهُ

Ḥadīth 67

عَنْ أَبِي الدَّرْدَاءِ رَضِيَ اللهُ عَنْهُ قَالَ: سَمِعْتُ أَبَا الْقَاسِمِ صَلَّى اللهُ عَلَيْهِ وَسَلَّمَ يَقُولُ: إِنَّ اللهَ قَالَ: يَا عِيسَى إِنِّي بَاعِثٌ مِنْ بَعْدِكَ أُمَّةً، إِنْ أَصَابَهُمْ مَا يُحِبُّونَ حَمِدُوا اللهَ، وَإِنْ أَصَابَهُمْ مَا يَكْرَهُونَ احْتَسَبُوا وَصَبَرُوا، وَلَا حِلْمَ وَلَا عِلْمَ. فَقَالَ: يَا رَبِّ، كَيْفَ يَكُونُ هَذَا لَهُمْ وَلَا حِلْمَ وَلَا عِلْمَ؟ قَالَ: أُعْطِيهِمْ مِنْ حِلْمِي وَعِلْمِي.

(رواه الحاكم في المستدرك وقال صحيح على شرط البخاري ووافقه الذهبي)

Abū 'l-Dardā' رَضِيَ اللهُ عَنْهُ narrates:

I heard Abū 'l-Qāsim[97] (the Messenger of Allah) صَلَّى اللهُ عَلَيْهِ وَسَلَّمَ saying, "Indeed, Allah says, 'O ʿĪsa, verily I will send

97 A *kunyah* (epithet or appellation) of the Prophet صَلَّى اللهُ عَلَيْهِ وَسَلَّمَ

after you such a nation that if they attain what they desire, then they will give praise and express gratitude. And if they experience what they dislike, then they will anticipate its reward and have patience, [and they will do this] without any forbearance or knowledge.' ʿĪsa then asks, 'My Lord, how will it be such, when they will have neither forbearance nor knowledge?' Allah says, 'I will bestow upon them from My forbearance and My knowledge.'"

(Ḥākim)

Commentary

The lofty status of the Ummah of Muḥammad ﷺ is made manifest in this ḥadīth. Allah ﷻ is extolling the virtue of this Ummah to the great Prophet of Allah—ʿĪsa ؑ. It shows that this Ummah has been granted this lofty status due to their patience upon calamities and gratitude for bounties.

It has been mentioned in one ḥadīth that the quality of the Ummah of Muḥammad ﷺ is "*ḥammādūn*" (those who praise Allah excessively). The name of the Prophet ﷺ is Aḥmad (the praised one), who will be carrying the Liwāʾ l-Ḥamd (the Banner of Praise) under which all of the believers will take shelter. Thus, this attribute and virtue is so great that it has become the identity and salient feature of this Ummah.

In another ḥadīth narrated by Aḥmad in his *Musnad*: "I am amazed by the decree of Allah for a believer, that when he is bestowed goodness, he praises Allah and thanks Him. And when he is afflicted, then he also praises Allah and is patient."

In a ḥadīth narrated by Ṭabarānī on the authority of Ibn ʿAbbās ⬥, it is stated that the first of those who are called to Paradise are the *ḥammādūn* - those who praise and thank Allah excessively in both good and bad conditions.

Lastly, we learn that patience and gratitude can only be achieved through Allah's bestowal and enablement (*tawfīq*); without this we would not be able to achieve anything.

After studying the extent of struggle and difficulty that the Beloved of Allah ⬥ underwent, there should be no doubt left in anyone's mind regarding the reality of trials and tribulations. They are nothing but a manifestation of Allah's love for His slave and are meant to elevate his rank and expiate his sins.

Here I conclude this blessed compilation in the month of Shawwāl, 1437 AH. May Allah send His most virtuous blessings and complete peace upon His Messenger ﷺ. I ask Allah ﷻ to spread the benefit of this compilation to this world and the next. And I ask that He make it a means of my salvation on the Day of Resurrection.

﴿يَوْمَ لَا يَنفَعُ مَالٌ وَلَا بَنُونَ ۝ إِلَّا مَنْ أَتَى ٱللَّهَ بِقَلْبٍ سَلِيمٍ﴾

"A Day wherein neither wealth nor offspring shall be of benefit, except for the one who brings to Allah a purified heart."

(Qurʾān 26:88–89)

May the Peace, Blessings and Salutations of Allah be upon the Master of the Messengers and the Leader of the People of Taqwā ﷺ, and upon his Family and Companions.

And we end our supplication with all praise and thanks to Allah, the Lord of all the Worlds.

Notes